"Michael A. Tompkins book, *OCD:*  a very helpful resource for those su disorder. In clear, direct language, T stand the nature of OCD, what trea right therapist, and how to work effectively toward coping difficult problem. People with OCD and their families will find this book to be useful."

> —Robert L. Leahy, PhD, director of the American Institute
> for Cognitive Therapy

"What a terrific book for individuals who have the very real illness of OCD, whether or not they have started treatment. This highly readable and practical book is also an important resource for families and friends who don't understand this often mystifying disorder or know what to do to help. I recommend it highly!"

> —Judith S. Beck, PhD, president of the Beck Institute for
> Cognitive Behavior Therapy and clinical associate
> professor of psychology at the University of Pennsylvania

"*OCD: A Guide for the Newly Diagnosed* gives those who have been recently diagnosed with OCD a head start on treatment. It addresses their and their families' many questions and worries triggered by the diagnosis. Thereby, immediate support and anxiety reduction are available. In addition, the guide offers clinicians a wealth of information that can be readily made available to their patients. I strongly recommend this book to patients, families, and mental health professionals."

> —Paul R. Munford, PhD, clinical psychologist and director of
> the Cognitive Behavior Therapy Center for OCD and
> Anxiety in San Rafael, CA

OCD

A GUIDE *for*
THE NEWLY
DIAGNOSED

Michael A. Tompkins, PhD

New Harbinger Publications, Inc.

Publisher's Note

Care has been taken to confirm the accuracy of the information presented and to describe generally accepted practices. However, the authors, editors, and publisher are not responsible for errors or omissions or for any consequences from application of the information in this book and make no warranty, express or implied, with respect to the contents of the publication.

The authors, editors, and publisher have exerted every effort to ensure that any drug selection and dosage set forth in this text are in accordance with current recommendations and practice at the time of publication. However, in view of ongoing research, changes in government regulations, and the constant flow of information relating to drug therapy and drug reactions, the reader is urged to check the package insert for each drug and consult with their health care provider for any change in indications and dosage and for added warnings and precautions. This is particularly important when the recommended agent is a new or infrequently employed drug.

Some drugs and medical devices presented in this publication may have Food and Drug Administration (FDA) clearance for limited use in restricted research settings. It is the responsibility of the health care provider to ascertain the FDA status of each drug or device planned for use in their clinical practice.

Distributed in Canada by Raincoast Books

Copyright © 2012 by Michael Tompkins
New Harbinger Publications, Inc.
5674 Shattuck Avenue
Oakland, CA 94609
www.newharbinger.com

Cover design by Amy Shoup; Text design by Michele Waters-Kermes;
Acquired by Melissa Kirk; Edited by Elisabeth Beller

Library of Congress Cataloging-in-Publication Data

Tompkins, Michael A.
OCD : a guide for the newly diagnosed / Michael A. Tompkins.
   p. cm.
Includes bibliographical references.
ISBN 978-1-60882-017-7 (pbk.) -- ISBN 978-1-60882-018-4 (pdf e-book)
1. Obsessive-compulsive disorder--Popular works. I. Title.
RC533.T66 2012
616.85'227--dc23
                                    2011039655

Printed in the United States of America

14   13   12

10   9   8   7   6   5   4   3   2   1   First printing

For Luann

CONTENTS

FOREWORD

In the vernacular of the mental health world, I am an *OCD consumer*, which is to say, I am someone who has undergone treatment for obsessive compulsive disorder. That Michael Tompkins would turn to me, a consumer, and not one of his many esteemed colleagues to write this foreword speaks volumes about the book you are holding in your hands. It says, loudly and clearly, "Let's get practical about OCD and its treatment. Let's cut to the chase about what people with OCD most need to know about this disorder and how to recover from it"—how refreshing!

As someone who spent years struggling with and seeking treatment for an affliction that neither I nor my first two therapists understood, I know firsthand the importance of all three of the very practical objectives Dr. Tompkins spells out and pursues in this book: *understanding*, *support*, and *education*. And as someone who was fortunate enough to have found all of these, I can say with confidence that the sense of hope Dr. Tompkins conveys is very real. I am living proof that someone who once battled severe OCD can regain his or her life. Whereas at my worst, I could barely leave my house, today I am a successful radio news anchor and mental health advocate, traveling coast to coast, generally unhindered by the obsessions and compulsions that once plagued me. But the "way out," as Dr. Tompkins describes recovery, is not easy. It is a road filled with countless hazards and steep uphill stretches. And—having learned this the hard way—I appreciate very much that this book makes clear that there are no shortcuts.

Over the past several years, I've come to share what you might call a "tough love" message in my OCD outreach, reminding my fellow consumers that, ultimately, the success or failure of their recoveries lies largely in their own hands. It's a harsh reality, perhaps, but an undeniable one. Dr. Tompkins reinforces this in every chapter ahead; but he also goes one very significant step further, offering a series of practical tools, suggestions, and resources for individuals with OCD and their loved ones to use at every turn. So when he talks about the value of understanding OCD, he provides the scientific background, personal anecdotes, and vocabulary necessary to do so. When he speaks of the need to get a correct diagnosis, he describes in detail what to expect during the evaluation process. And when he stresses the importance of finding the right therapist, he suggests where they can be found. In this fashion, Dr. Tompkins empowers his readers, page by page, to regain control of those aspects of their lives that OCD has likely stolen from them.

My own personal journey to OCD recovery has been an especially circuitous one. I stumbled my way through the mental health system, asking poor questions of the first two therapists I saw, accepting misdiagnoses for far too long, and refusing to do the hard work of OCD treatment once I found my way to it. I can't help but wonder now what my journey might have looked like had I been fortunate enough to have had a copy of this very book at my disposal all those years ago. I'll never know for sure, but of this I am certain: the extremely clear roadmap Dr. Tompkins has developed and shares here can serve as a powerful guide not only for newly diagnosed OCD consumers, but also for their friends and relatives and even therapists. Whichever *you* are, I hope that you'll take in all the practical wisdom this book has to offer.

—Jeff Bell
Author, *Rewind, Replay, Repeat:*
A Memoir of Obsessive-Compulsive Disorder

Acknowledgments

This book would not have been possible without the support and encouragement of many people.

I would like to thank my colleagues at the San Francisco Bay Area Center for Cognitive Therapy, beginning with Jacqueline B. Persons, director of the Center, for her continued support of this book and the others she has nurtured along the way. I want to thank other Center colleagues (Joan Davidson, Janie Hong, Daniel Weiner, and Daniela Owen) for their continued support of my professional development.

I wish to thank my editor, Melissa Kirk, for her steady guidance through the process of writing the book and for her tolerance of my missteps along the way. I look forward to our working together on other projects in the future. I thank Jess Beebe, editorial manager, and Nicola Skidmore, associate editor, both at New Harbinger, for improving the quality of the book in general.

In particular, I want to thank my wife, Luann L. DeVoss, and our daughters, Madeleine and Olivia, for their unwavering support of another book project. It is impossible to imagine doing this without them by my side.

Finally, I wish to acknowledge those who have taught me the most about this difficult condition we call obsessive-compulsive disorder—those who suffer with the problem as well as the family members and friends who love them. Your courage and determination to better your situations continues to inspire me and enrich my life.

INTRODUCTION

Jason has always been "meticulous" and, as he often remarked, liked to get his day off "on the right foot." When Jason awakened, he would get out of bed on the right side only. Most mornings, he did this only once, but over the last few months, he'd started to feel very uncomfortable the first time and would have to get back in bed and get out again several times until he felt that he had "gotten it right." He would then brush his teeth, carefully brushing each tooth front, back, and top repeatedly, beginning with the bottom-most rear tooth and moving clockwise. It was starting to take Jason well over thirty minutes to brush his teeth, and many times when he finished, his gums would be sore and bleeding. Then Jason would begin his showering routine, which he did in a meticulous manner too.

Jason wasn't afraid anything bad would happen if he didn't do things in a certain way; he just felt uncomfortable unless he did them in a specific way, and this discomfort didn't go away until he got it right. Jason tried to limit these types of routines, but it seemed like they were spreading. Now he had to make his bed a certain way and close the doors and cabinets just the right way or he felt extremely uncomfortable and he would repeatedly make and unmake the bed and close and open the doors until he felt right. The basement door was particularly frustrating for him because it was a hollow door and he did not like the way it sounded when he closed it—it just didn't sound right. Jason's morning routine now took him over two hours to complete, and he was getting up earlier and earlier to make more time for it. Even so, he was getting to work an hour late, sometimes more, several times a week. His supervisor spoke to him about his tardiness, which didn't help. Now he was anxious about losing his job and, along with getting less sleep, he was having even more difficulty speeding things along in the morning. He had started to take off days from work to catch up on his sleep or if it looked like he'd be several hours late.

When Jason noticed he was having trouble getting to bed at a reasonable time because he now needed to do things just right in order to get to sleep, he panicked. He thought he was going crazy—really losing it. His family and friends told him that perhaps the stress at work was making him so anxious, but when he thought about it, he realized that it was his routines that were adding stress to his job, not the job itself. Still, Jason didn't know what was happening to him until he went to the Employee

Assistance Program representative at work who told him that he might have OCD.

SHAME, FEAR, AND DENIAL

Often, people with obsessive-compulsive disorder (OCD) know that something is amiss but are reluctant to seek help. This is unfortunate because we know that most people who seek and participate fully in treatment improve, sometimes greatly.

There are a number of reasons you may be reluctant to seek treatment for your OCD. You may feel ashamed by what you think of as the bizarre nature of your obsessive thoughts. You may believe that having the thoughts you do means you are an immoral or terrible person and so you feel ashamed and reluctant to tell people about these thoughts. You may have tried many times to stop your washing or checking rituals because you know that the washing or checking is excessive, but you feel powerless to stop. It's not easy to tell someone that you are aware your behavior doesn't make sense but that you have to do it anyway.

In addition to the shame you feel, you may be afraid to seek help for your OCD, fearing that you will lose your job, marriage, or children if people find out you have OCD. A former client told me that she suffered for years with obsessions that she might molest her children. She did not tell her parents or even her husband about these thoughts because she feared that they would tell the authorities and they would take away her children. You may have read something about the treatment of your OCD, particularly about exposure, and now you worry that this will only make your symptoms worse or truly create the catastrophe that you are working so hard to prevent. Fear, like shame, may cause you to attempt to suppress your obsessions (try to keep them out of your mind), which only makes things worse. As you try not to think about the disgusting or terrifying thoughts or images that come into your mind, you realize that they are coming with greater frequency and intensity. This, in turn, makes you believe that you might be going crazy or that what you fear may indeed be true.

Given the shame and fear that you may feel about your OCD symptoms, it is natural that you might deny or minimize the severity of your symptoms. Even though you are fully aware that your thoughts are irrational and your compulsions are excessive, you might find it difficult to admit that you are having a problem.

THE WAY OUT

The way out of the shame, fear, and denial begins with awareness and education about your OCD. It is essential that the person with OCD (and his or her family) increase his or her understanding of the condition and become knowledgeable about available treatment options and resources. The way out also depends on finding the right treatment and the right treatment provider. The objective of this book is to show the way out, through understanding, support, and education.

HOW TO USE THIS BOOK

This book is a primer for people recently diagnosed with obsessive-compulsive disorder who want basic information about the condition and its treatment. Throughout the book, I will use the terms "obsessive-compulsive disorder," "OCD," and "condition" interchangeably to describe the disorder. Although the book does not extensively cite research findings, I have based the book on the extensive research available, which goes back to the investigators who first described the condition well over fifty years ago. In addition, I have tried to stick to research about the condition and its treatment that is widely accepted by most expert investigators rather than presenting information that is either speculative or incomplete.

I have organized the book along the path most people take when first diagnosed with the condition:

- *Chapter 1: What Is Obsessive-Compulsive Disorder?* The first step is to search for accurate information about the condition and its treatment. This chapter presents basic information about OCD, including its prevalence, its onset, and current theories about what may cause it.

- *Chapter 2: Get the Right Diagnosis.* For those who have not yet received a formal diagnosis or have self-diagnosed OCD, this chapter describes the process of seeking and getting an accurate diagnosis, which is the starting point for an effective treatment. Not all mental health professionals are familiar with OCD and some may miss the diagnosis, particularly if symptoms are more subtle than the classic symptoms of washing and checking. This chapter guides you through the diagnostic process, explaining what a mental health professional needs to know to give you the right diagnosis and how to describe your symptoms accurately.

• *Chapter 3: Find the Right Treatment.* The next step in the process is to find the right treatment. This is not as easy a process as you might think and is in fact one of the most frustrating aspects for those newly diagnosed with the condition and their family members. This chapter describes the most effective treatments for the condition and presents other treatments, less well understood but used at times for more serious symptoms.

• *Chapter 4: Put Together Your Treatment Team.* Once you find the right treatment for your condition, this chapter walks you through the process of finding your treatment team. The team may consist of prescribers, psychotherapists experienced in the psychological treatment of OCD, support groups, or other team members who may be helpful for your particular situation. This chapter describes how (and where) to find a knowledgeable therapist to treat your OCD, how to get the most out of every treatment session, how to pay for treatment, and how to deal with other issues that can occur over the course of treatment.

- *Chapter 5: Find the Right Support.* This chapter describes how to seek appropriate support from the important people in your life and from additional sources of support, such as face-to-face and online support groups.

- *Chapter 6: Develop a Recovery Attitude.* This chapter describes perhaps the single most important feature needed to manage OCD now and for the long term—a recovery attitude. The chapter describes the essential features of a recovery attitude and explains why this is key during treatment and after treatment ends. A recovery attitude includes healthy habits such as getting enough exercise, proper nutrition, and sleep to enhance both your general health and your resilience when managing your OCD on a day-to-day basis.

- *Chapter 7: Unhealthy Coping and Other Psychological Issues.* People who struggle with OCD may at times turn to unhealthy ways to cope with their suffering, such as alcohol and drugs. This chapter describes what to watch out for and how to get help for problems with substance use. It also describes other psychological issues or conditions, such as depression, that can arise when someone has OCD.

- *Chapter 8: Workplace or School Issues.* This chapter describes what happens when OCD begins to affect performance in the workplace or in school. This chapter offers suggestions for what to do if this is happening and describes your legal rights in the workplace and the classroom.

- *Resources and References.* For those wanting more detailed information, I have added a list of references and other resources at the end of the book, including websites and organizations that may be of interest to those with the condition as well as to their friends, family members, and mental health professionals.

Although I have written the book mainly for people with OCD, I hope that family members, friends, psychotherapists, physicians, employers, and coworkers find the book helpful too. At times, family members and friends are more aware that something is amiss than the sufferer. Many people with OCD manage the condition through its ups and downs for years and seek treatment only when symptoms create more distress and disruption in their lives than they can continue to tolerate. I hope this book reassures those of you with OCD that there is help and that it provides a useful resource for you, your family members, and friends, for many years to come.

CHAPTER 1

WHAT IS OBSESSIVE-COMPULSIVE DISORDER?

Last week, I was in the grocery store for over three hours. I kept arranging the cans on the shelves to make sure that all the labels faced out perfectly—every can on every shelf. It's crazy, I know, but I'd still be doing this if an employee hadn't threatened to call the police if I didn't leave. My wife does all the shopping now.

—Jamaal

Obsessive-compulsive disorder is an anxiety disorder, and people who suffer with OCD—like those who suffer with phobias, panic disorder, or social phobia—experience intense anxiety or discomfort that they cannot effectively control. People with OCD experience either obsessions or compulsions or both, and these symptoms cause significant distress or affect their ability to function in their daily lives. People who suffer with OCD are aware that something is amiss and that they are thinking and acting irrationally at times. However, they are not able to change their thinking and behavior, even though they may be rational and reasonable in every other way.

In this chapter, I define obsessions and compulsions and describe the common subtypes of OCD. I describe the relationship between obsessions and compulsions that contributes to the maintenance of the symptoms over time. I briefly describe the prevalence, onset, and course of OCD and present current theories about its possible causes.

WHAT IS AN OBSESSION?

An *obsession* is a recurrent, persistent, and intrusive thought, image, or impulse that is unacceptable and unwanted. We call thoughts like these intrusive because they intrude—not ease—into our awareness and get our attention. Someone with OCD recognizes that an obsession is his own thought and not a thought introduced from another person or other outside force. This is an important distinction because some people with other mental illnesses may believe that others have inserted thoughts into their minds or that others are controlling their thoughts. In addition, an obsession in the case of OCD is different from how people use the term in everyday life. People may tell you that a friend is obsessed with sports or his new girlfriend to describe how the friend is very interested in and spends a lot of time thinking about something or someone. However, this is not like a true obsession; here the friend enjoys this mental activity and, therefore, does not attempt to get the thought out of his mind.

People with OCD may experience fewer obsessions when an interesting activity distracts them. Because there may be no distractions during those few minutes between lights out and sleep, bedtime can be particularly difficult for people with OCD. Similarly, people may have more obsessions when they are bored or even when on vacation because they are not distracted by work activities. Because the obsessions are unpleasant, the person experiencing them usually attempts to push the obsessions out of awareness by trying to think about something else or by engaging his or her attention in an activity.

TYPES OF OBSESSIONS

There are three common types or themes of obsessions: aggressive/harm, sexual, and religious or moral.

Aggressive/Harm

The most common are *aggressive/harm obsessions*: thoughts of harming or harm coming to others or self. For example, a young man is fearful that he might lose control and push someone in front of an oncoming car or train, and a woman is terrified she might smother her sleeping children. Some aggressive/harm obsessions can be less scary but nonetheless unwanted: A young man has thoughts that he might accidentally impregnate a woman passenger sitting next to him on the bus, or a teenage girl is terrified that she might say something that hurts her best friend's feelings.

Sexual

The second most common theme for obsessions is unwanted sexual thoughts. *Sexual obsessions* typically include images or thoughts of disgusting or unacceptable sexual desires or acts, such as thoughts about sleeping with a parent or sibling or of molesting children. As with those who have aggressive obsessions, people with sexual obsessions may also fear they will lose control and act on these repugnant desires or thoughts.

Religious or Moral

Religious or moral obsessions is the third common theme for obsessions; these take the form of unwanted blasphemous thoughts, such as a young man who thinks profane words when he prays silently to himself or has obscene thoughts about sacred religious figures.

WHAT IS A COMPULSION?

A *compulsion* is a deliberate and purposeful behavior that the person with OCD feels driven to carry out, sometimes many times. Most of the time, but not always, the person must carry out the compulsion in a rigid and set pattern of steps that have a beginning and an end. Experts call a compulsion like this a *ritual*. Typically, someone with OCD carries out a compulsion because he believes that the compulsion will prevent harm or other bad things from happening to him or to others. For example, a twenty-five-year-old graduate student repeatedly washed his hands when he thought he had touched something that might have the AIDS virus on it. When he washed, he did it in a specific and elaborate way, beginning with the small finger on his left hand and moving up and down the inside of the finger to the next.

However, for some people, the goal of the compulsion is to lessen discomfort rather than to prevent harm. They will tell you that nothing bad will happen if they don't complete the compulsion but that they just won't feel right or complete if they don't complete it. For example, a young female attorney had a compulsion to touch with her left hand—in the same way and with the same pressure—anything she touched with her right hand. In addition, she felt the need to touch her foot to the floor with the same pressure on each foot or, if she bumped something with her left side, she had to touch it with her right side and in the same way. This urge to put things right leads to compulsions to order and arrange. These can take many hours to perform and include tasks like arranging the clothes in the closet or ordering the items on a desk. Compulsions like these are not only distressing but frustrating because the person often must complete the task before moving on or starting a new task or activity.

As mentioned, because the content of most obsessions is distressing, people tend to resist or try to push these thoughts or images out of their awareness. People tend to resist the compulsions too, at least at first, because the compulsions themselves can be time consuming or distressing. Most people would not volunteer to stand at the sink and wash every finger on each hand many times, using scalding hot water, for thirty or forty minutes. However, over time, people tend to resist their compulsions less often, in part, because some compulsions take so little time that it seems easier to do them than to resist.

TYPES OF COMPULSIONS

When people think about OCD, they typically think about people who repeatedly and excessively check and clean. Checking and cleaning and washing compulsions are the most common ones for most people with OCD, followed by ordering and arranging, mental rituals, repeating, counting, and hoarding.

Checking

People with checking compulsions are trying to decrease the likelihood that some harm or misfortune will befall them or others. They check that they have locked doors and windows at home and then check again, just in case they didn't lock it the first time. They check and recheck that electrical appliances are off. They check and recheck that they have locked their vehicles and set the parking brake. One man, an accountant, checked his calculations twenty, thirty, or forty times, which caused him to work late into the night. He checked and rechecked e-mails before he sent them. He even made lists and developed other elaborate strategies to reassure himself that, in fact, he had checked the e-mails and calculations.

Cleaning and Washing

People with cleaning compulsions have an intense fear and dread of contamination and, through cleaning and washing, they hope to prevent the perceived threat, danger, or discomfort. I use the term "contamination," rather than "feeling dirty," because feelings of contamination can include more than feeling dirty. They can also include feelings of disgust or other unpleasant emotions such as guilt or shame. Most often, people with OCD clean and wash to remove the *feeling* of contamination after physical contact with objects or materials perceived as dangerous, dirty, or disgusting. People can quickly remove true dirt with some soap and water. Removing the "feeling" of dirt can take much longer. Adding to the disruption caused by cleaning and washing compulsions is the extent to which people will go to avoid coming in contact with "contaminated" materials or situations. For example, some people will avoid public restrooms, if possible, and when not possible, will use a variety of strategies to minimize contamination—opening doors with their feet, standing over the toilet rather than sitting on it, waiting to rush in or out of the restroom after someone else to avoid touching the door handle, and so on.

Feelings of contamination are not limited to contact with a physical object. People with OCD can feel contaminated by a thought or image as well. For example, whenever she was spending time with her family, a nineteen-year-old woman felt the need to shower any time she thought about having sex with her boyfriend. Another woman felt contaminated any time she thought about a homeless person and would then wash her hands repeatedly.

Putting Things Right

People with ordering and arranging compulsions experience extreme distress when things are not as they should be, and, may not be able to delay the ordering or arranging compulsion for even a few minutes. People order or arrange objects for one of two reasons: (1) they believe that if they do not, some terrible disaster will befall them or others or (2) they simply need to put things right rather than to prevent something bad from happening. Their discomfort is not fear but a sense that they don't feel at ease or quite right. To address this feeling, people will arrange their books, clothes, or other possessions in a particular order or way. They will arrange cans on grocery shelves or in the pantry at home. They will hang clothes and arrange shoes in a particular order in the closet. This can take many hours, and the person dealing with OCD may not be able to move on or begin a new task or activity until he or she has put things right. In addition, people can become extremely upset when others interrupt or disrupt this compulsion and often must then begin the process again.

Repeating and Hoarding

Similarly, people with OCD may repeat actions to avoid a feared consequence, such as rewriting a check to avoid making a mistake or turning a light switch on and off repeatedly until it feels just right. Counting compulsions include counting breaths, counting eye blinks, and taking steps to avoid odd numbers.

Close to 22 percent of those with OCD have some hoarding and saving compulsions (Abramowitz 2006). They collect and keep empty grocery bags, envelopes and all manner of paper, or excessive amounts of items for some purpose or interest, such as art supplies, cosmetics, or small appliances.

Compulsions by Proxy

At times, people with OCD will get others to do their compulsions for them. A husband might ask his wife to wipe down the counters carefully or insist that she check that they have locked the doors and turned off the electrical appliances. A woman might insist that her husband repeat a phrase in a certain way or that he arrange the clothes in his closet exactly the way she does. Many times, family members agree to help with the compulsions because it is often quicker and easier to do it for the loved one than to wait for him or her to do it. In addition, people with OCD may enlist family members to help them avoid triggering their obsessions and distress by asking them to open the door to a public bathroom for them or to avoid using certain words or phrases that tend to trigger unpleasant obsessions.

Mini-compulsions

When people with OCD are not able to complete the full compulsion, they may resort to mini-compulsions. For example, rather than leaping up in a meeting to go wash his hands, a software engineer repeatedly wiped his hands on paper towels or on his pants. The objective of a mini-compulsion is the same as a full compulsion—to reduce anxiety or discomfort—and the person usually uses a mini-compulsion to get through the moment, to get by until such time as she can engage in the full compulsion. A quick glance at the door rather than walking back to check the lock or shortening a "protective" phrase from several words to a single word would also be a mini-compulsion.

Mental Compulsions

A large number of people with OCD have mental compulsions. Mental compulsions are mental acts, such as repeating a prayer or a special phrase to oneself, aimed at preventing some feared consequence. Because mental compulsions are thoughts, as are obsessions, many people with OCD may find it difficult to distinguish between a mental compulsion and an obsession. However, like behavioral compulsions, people deliberately perform mental compulsions to decrease anxiety or distress. Obsessions, on the other hand, are not under the control of the person. They are unwanted and involuntary thoughts that come into awareness suddenly and without forethought.

Seeking Reassurance

Many people with OCD seek reassurance from other people, most often from family members or even a therapist. People seek reassurance when they doubt that they have performed a task or are not certain about something. "Did I do it correctly? Do I need to check the locks again? Is that spot on my cheek cancer?" are the kinds of questions that people feel compelled to ask. When the friend or family member reassures the person with OCD, she feels less anxious or distressed for a while, but soon the doubts and questions return. Adding to the frustration is that, most times, the person with OCD knows the answer to the question and, therefore, knows the answer she will receive. The objective of the question, however, is not to gather information but to lessen anxiety.

OTHER NEUTRALIZATION STRATEGIES

Most people with OCD use other overt or covert *neutralization strategies* that are not, strictly speaking, compulsions or rituals because the aim of these strategies is not necessarily to prevent some unacceptable outcome. The objective of these neutralization strategies is to control, remove, or prevent the obsessions themselves. They include overanalyzing or trying to convince oneself of the unimportance of the thought, replacing one thought with another, distracting oneself, and suppressing a thought. Like compulsions and rituals, these neutralization strategies are deliberate and are used to escape the distress created by an obsession.

HOW THE OCD BALL KEEPS ROLLING

Although we don't know what causes OCD or, as the saying goes, gets the ball rolling, we do have some idea about what *keeps* it rolling. Actually, the factors that keep the ball rolling may be more important to you right now because if you understand them, you may be able to slow that rolling ball and perhaps even stop it.

Triggers

A *trigger* is an external or internal event that sets off an obsession or a feeling of discomfort or distress. External triggers are objects or situations in the environment that start the ball rolling. For example, every time a young attorney saw a bus approaching as he walked to his office, he had the obsession, "Did I push someone in front of the bus?" The bus was the external object that triggered his obsession. Most people are very aware of these external triggers but often less aware of *internal triggers:* mental events, like memories, that can trigger an obsession. For example, every time a woman remembered her mother, who had died in a car accident, the memory triggered the obsession that perhaps the woman had caused the accident in some way.

Intrusive Thoughts

We all experience intrusive thoughts all day long. Out of nowhere, we might have the thought of a childhood friend and wonder what he is doing. We might sit at our desks and daydream, our minds flitting from one thought to another. As I type a letter to a colleague, I am surprised when an image of a glazed donut enters my mind. An *intrusive thought* is any thought, image, memory, or mental event that enters your awareness. In a sense, when you are aware of a thought, it is because it has elbowed its way into awareness by pushing aside other thoughts or distractions. People without OCD have intrusive thoughts, but they can easily dismiss them, in part because they have not labeled such thoughts as dangerous, harmful, or "bad" in some way.

Faulty Appraisals

A thought is just a thought. In other words, what makes a thought significant is the meaning you attach to it. When you appraise a thought as highly significant, revealing, threatening, or catastrophic, the harmless thought causes you to feel anxious or upset in some way. People with OCD fall prey to six irrational beliefs that can transform a thought into an obsession.

1. *People with OCD tend to overestimate the likelihood and costs of negative events.* In fact, people with OCD tend to assume a situation is dangerous unless they can guarantee that is completely safe. For example, June, an experienced sales manager, overestimated the likelihood that she would miss some important piece of information in e-mails she received, which would lead her to lose her job and never find employment again. This overestimation of the likelihood and costs of a simple mistake like this caused her to repeatedly check each of the one hundred or so e-mails she sent each day.

2. *People with OCD believe that they have the power to cause or prevent certain disastrous events and, in that way, are responsible for what happens to them or to others.* This inflated sense of responsibility leads people with OCD to feel anxious, particularly when they assume responsibility for events over which they have little influence, such as protecting a loved one from all harm.

3. *People with OCD are apt to assign too much importance to their random thoughts.* For example, some people with OCD believe that their intrusive thoughts are statements about their personality or character. Therefore, a repugnant sexual thought means the person thinking it is sick or weird, or an intrusive thought about harming someone means

the thinker is unstable or evil. This tendency to assign too much importance to intrusive thoughts can lead to what is termed *thought-action fusion* (TAF). TAF refers to the irrational belief that thinking about doing something bad or wrong is the same as doing it. A second form of TAF assumes that thinking about something bad happening increases the likelihood that the bad thing will happen. These two irrational beliefs, as you might gather, can create intense feelings of fear and shame.

4. *People with OCD believe that it is both possible and necessary to maintain complete control over their thoughts.* Anyone who has tried to clear his mind or not think about something specific—like white bears—realizes how futile an effort this is. The belief that you not only *should* but *can* control certain thoughts can cause you to try to resist the obsessions—that is, push them from your awareness.

5. *People with OCD often believe that it is both important and possible to be absolutely (100 percent) certain that a bad thing won't happen.* The multitude of bad things that are "possible" but not likely terrify people with OCD, who then focus their energies on eliminating even the smallest risk. Whereas it is possible to contract tuberculosis from someone who coughs on the sidewalk fifty feet away from

you, because anything is possible, it is highly unlikely. The need to be certain—absolutely and completely certain—leads people with OCD to resort to extreme and irrational degrees of avoidance and senseless and distressing compulsions.

6.   *People with OCD have great difficulty tolerating any mistake or imperfection of their own, no matter how small.* This leads to relentless efforts to avoid mistakes, such as checking and rechecking whether they filled out a form correctly or filed a paper where it belongs. In addition, they may repeat routine activities, such as making beds or hanging clothes in the closet, until it feels "just right," which achieves some internal sense of completion or perfection. They believe that if something is worth doing, it is worth doing right, but to them "right" means "perfect," and they continue to work and overwork tasks well beyond what is reasonable.

Selective Attention

Once you appraise a thought as threatening in some way, you are going to pay attention to it. This is a natural and automatic feature of the body's danger detection system. Just as when you fear that there are threats in your environment (dangerous objects or situations) and hypervigilantly scan your surroundings, when you fear that there are threats in your mind (dangerous thoughts), you scan your consciousness. Only the difference is whereas you can't conjure a bear in the forest, for instance, your mind has the capability to create precisely what you fear. So you go looking for these thoughts and—guess what? You find them.

Discomfort

Once an obsession enters your awareness, you feel uncomfortable. People with OCD experience many forms of discomfort, not just anxiety. Some people describe the discomfort as feeling ill at ease. Others feel tense or out of sorts. Still others feel intensely guilty or ashamed when the obsession comes into their minds.

Compulsions and Other Neutralization Strategies

In OCD, discomfort drives the compulsive urge to carry out a behavior or some other action to lessen the discomfort or prevent the bad thing from happening. Rituals, mental compulsions, and reassurance seeking are strategies people with OCD use to neutralize the distress they experience. In addition, the neutralization strategies people with OCD use to escape the perceived danger prevent them from learning that they aren't in danger at all. For example, the man with contamination fears who washes his hands many times after he touches a doorknob doesn't have an opportunity to learn that he doesn't fall ill when he doesn't wash after touching doorknobs.

Reduction of Discomfort

When someone with OCD carries out the compulsion or neutralization strategy in the required way, she feels relief. If she felt anxious, she feels less anxious after she completes the compulsion. If she felt guilty or ashamed, she feels less guilty or ashamed. However, the relief is temporary and, at times, requires great effort to achieve. For that reason, even when a person is able to lessen her discomfort, she may feel frustrated and demoralized by the experience. Furthermore, although compulsions typically lessen discomfort, they can, over time, begin to work less well, which increases the amount of time a person engages in or adds features to the compulsion.

Avoidance and Concealment

Most people with OCD avoid certain objects or situations that trigger their obsessions. People who compulsively check will avoid situations that they see as unsafe or that increase their sense of responsibility. A person with OCD also tries to conceal the content and frequency of obsessions for fear that people will think he is weird, dangerous, or sick.

PREVALENCE, ONSET, AND COURSE

The likelihood that someone will develop OCD during his or her life is about 2.6 percent, which makes OCD a relatively rare condition (Karno et al. 1988). However, of those who do develop OCD, around half have severe symptoms.

The percentage of men and women who develop OCD is about the same, although children with OCD are more typically boys than girls. OCD usually develops in adolescence or early adulthood (before the age of twenty-five) and develops earlier in males than in females. Most times, the onset of OCD is gradual, over many months or years; however, some people can experience a sudden and dramatic onset of the symptoms. Even if the onset is gradual, stress can accelerate the course and intensify the symptoms. Common stressors include the loss of a job or relationship, death or illness of a loved one, childbirth, or marital problems. At times, people develop OCD following an episode of depression.

There may be periods in which the person has few if any symptoms for weeks, months, and sometimes years, followed by periods of intense symptoms. For roughly half of the people with OCD, obsessions and compulsions worsen over time until they are no longer able to manage the symptoms on their own.

CAUSES OF OBSESSIVE-COMPULSIVE DISORDER

We do not yet have a comprehensive theory that all investigators agree adequately explains what causes OCD. In this section, I briefly describe the most common theories for the cause of OCD.

Genetic or Biological Theories

A number of genetic studies suggest that there is a heritable factor in OCD (Pauls et al. 1995); however, this heritable factor appears to be quite nonspecific (Goldstein et al. 1994). At this time, studies support that people tend to inherit a general emotional sensitivity that can predispose them to develop some form of an anxiety or mood disorder, but the genetic contribution doesn't make someone more or less likely to develop OCD specifically.

Current biological theories propose that a biochemical imbalance in the brain causes OCD. Investigators have proposed that people with OCD may have inadequate levels of *serotonin* (a certain *neurotransmitter*, a chemical that carries messages in the brain). The primary support for this theory lies in the effectiveness of drugs that block serotonin *reuptake* (reabsorption), thereby increasing the level of serotonin in the brain and observing a decrease in OCD symptoms. (Collaborative Study Group 1991; Chouinard 1992). However, researchers have not demonstrated a consistent link between OCD and abnormalities in serotonin activity (Jenike et al. 1991). Researchers have suggested that *dopamine*, another neurotransmitter, may play a role in OCD (Insel et al. 1983) or that an autoimmune response that attacks the basal ganglia or another area of the brain may cause OCD in some people (Allen, Leonard, and Swedo 1995). The theory suggests that the immune system mistakes the basal ganglia or another area of the brain for something foreign and therefore attacks it. These theories are intriguing but require much more research to clarify what role, if any, these mechanisms may play in the cause of OCD.

Psychological Theories

Learning and behavioral theories assume that we all learn to fear things through some life experiences. We may learn to fear certain people, objects, or situations when we have a painful, threatening, or upsetting experience with them. We can also learn to be afraid of something by watching someone else have a painful or upsetting experience with an object or situation—or by just listening to someone talk about a frightening experience. You can also learn that a certain action or behavior, such as a compulsion, can decrease your anxiety, which thereby increases the likelihood that you will do the action again if you are anxious in the same way again. For example, if you enter a room that is hot and stuffy and adjust the thermostat down such that the room feels cool and comfortable, you are very likely to adjust the thermostat down again if you enter the room again the next day and find it hot and stuffy. In fact, you are apt to continue to adjust the thermostat, even if it does not cause the room to cool immediately, because it worked that one time. This learning or behavioral theory takes the same view of compulsions. If someone feels anxious or afraid about contamination, quickly washes or showers to rid herself of the contaminant, and then notices that her fear decreases, she is likely to wash again when she thinks she is contaminated.

Compulsions do decrease anxiety in the short term. This may explain why people with OCD hold on so tightly to rituals they know to be senseless: in part because in the past, it brought them some temporary relief.

Learning theory, however, fails to explain why so many people with OCD don't recall a painful or threatening experience from which they initially learned to fear a particular object or situation. In addition, learning theory cannot adequately explain why people with OCD learn to fear only certain things, such as dirt and germs. One explanation is that we all possess *prepared fears*, fears that we are "primed" to develop because they confer a biological or evolutionary advantage. For example, the tendency to fear snakes and the dark caused our early ancestors to avoid these objects or situations (or at least to approach them with caution) and thereby helped them live to see the next day and contribute to the gene pool.

The *cognitive theory* for OCD assumes that people with OCD have faulty beliefs and assumptions that contribute to their obsessive fears. This cognitive theory assumes that people with OCD tend to misinterpret common intrusive thoughts as threatening or unacceptable. I have described these irrational beliefs earlier in this chapter.

SUMMING UP

Because you are reading this book, you may have the impression that you may be one of the two to three million adults in the United States with OCD. However, an impression is not the same as a diagnosis. Now that you have learned a bit about OCD, the next step is to get the right diagnosis. The right diagnosis is the first step in your recovery from OCD.

CHAPTER 2

GET THE RIGHT
DIAGNOSIS

It started after my brother died. I started to worry that I would lose photos of him or letters he had written me— anything associated with him, really—little gifts he gave me when we were kids. I never threw anything away because I thought I might accidentally toss something of his away. In a few weeks, I had filled my apartment with paper and junk that, in the past, I would have tossed. I know it's crazy, but I once examined a single piece of notebook paper for over thirty minutes to make certain that something of my brother's wasn't stuck to the paper. I'd still be turning that piece of paper over and over if I hadn't asked my boyfriend to check it and tell me that I hadn't tucked something accidentally into some imagined crease in the paper.

—Kayla

After what you have read or heard about OCD, you may be pretty certain that you have the condition. However, a hunch is not the same as a diagnosis. Many times, people with OCD seek help but a professional misses the OCD diagnosis. Mental health professionals often diagnose people who have OCD with some other condition that they do not have. In this chapter, I describe the process of getting the right diagnosis. I begin by describing the criteria used to diagnose OCD and go on to describe the evaluation and treatment planning process. The chapter closes with some dos and don'ts about getting the right diagnosis.

DIAGNOSIS

Getting a correct diagnosis is not as easy as you may think. Many mental health professionals lack the training necessary to make a clear diagnosis of OCD; for that reason, many people will see more than one professional and may spend several years in the wrong treatment before receiving the correct diagnosis. In fact, it takes between seven and eight years from the time OCD begins for people to obtain the correct diagnosis and seek treatment (Rasmussen and Tsuang 1986). That's why it is so very important that you obtain the correct diagnosis and find the right treatment and mental health professional to provide that treatment. The sooner you find the correct treatment, the sooner you begin your recovery from OCD.

HOW A DIAGNOSIS CAN HELP

Let me be clear—you are much more than a diagnosis. You have interests, hobbies, and important personal values. You have loving family members and friends. Your neighbors may admire your ingenuity or work ethic. You may be the "go-to guy or gal" when friends and family are seeking wise counsel or help. A *diagnosis*, on the other hand, is just a description of signs and symptoms that mental health and medical professionals use to evaluate whether a condition is present or not. A *symptom* is a piece of subjective evidence of the condition—something the client or patient experiences but the professional cannot see. A *sign* is a piece of objective evidence of the condition—something the mental health professional can see. For example, if you go to your physician and tell her you are in pain, she will examine you. She will ask you where you feel pain, whether it is sharp or dull, and other questions about what you can feel but the physician cannot see. What you describe is a *symptom* of pain. As your physician examines you, you may flinch when she touches the painful area. Flinching is a *sign* of the pain.

When it comes to OCD, a mental health professional may observe some straightening or repeating compulsions during the evaluation, or you may tell her about your washing and cleaning compulsions, which are behaviors that others can observe. These are signs of your OCD. However, your obsessions—the distressing and intrusive thoughts, images, impulses, or doubts—are not visible to the mental health professional, and these are the symptoms of your OCD. Therefore, a diagnosis is just a series of signs and symptoms that the mental health professional will consider to determine whether or not you have OCD.

Getting a correct diagnosis is a time-consuming and, at times, uncomfortable process, in part because describing the signs and symptoms of what you are experiencing brings them all back to you. In addition, no diagnosis is perfect and your symptoms may not fit nicely into all the criteria for the condition. This can leave you and your mental health professional scratching your heads.

However, in spite of these reservations, there are several important benefits to hanging in there with a professional in order to get a correct diagnosis:

- A *diagnosis is the link to studies that identify the most effective treatment for OCD.* The best studies are randomized controlled trials that test a specific treatment against a placebo, the way researchers test whether a drug or medication is effective for a particular medical condition, such as high blood pressure or diabetes. Therefore, with a correct diagnosis, the mental health professional will be able to find and direct you to the best available treatment for your OCD. The diagnosis will also help the mental health professional direct you to other important information, such as how long a typical treatment lasts and how much benefit you might get from it. In other words, a correct diagnosis is your path to essential information about the appropriate treatment for your OCD.

- *When we put a name on something—as with a diagnosis—we open the door to finding important information about it.* Information is power, and an appropriate diagnosis can lead you to information about where you can find these treatments, as well as other resources, such as support groups or books and articles on the subject. I cover these and other topics later in the book, but you likely have started to gather information yourself through the library, bookstores, or the Internet.

- *Many times, an appropriate diagnosis helps your friends and family members understand what is going on with you.* Often, what friends and family members observe puzzles them, and they jump to the conclusion that you're lazy, crazy, or worse. With an appropriate diagnosis, you can direct them to solid information that will help them better understand your suffering. In addition, once friends and family members truly understand what's going on with you, they may want to help you find the correct help.

- *A correct diagnosis can help you find not only the appropriate treatment for your OCD but also some help paying for that treatment.* OCD is a *parity diagnosis*, which means that insurance companies must treat mental illnesses the same way they do physical illnesses. I will say more about paying for treatment in chapter 4 ("Put Together Your Treatment Team"), but the bottom line is that a parity diagnosis increases the likelihood that your insurance company will reimburse you for at least some of the OCD treatment.

DIAGNOSTIC CRITERIA FOR OBSESSIVE-COMPULSIVE DISORDER

Mental health professionals make the diagnosis of OCD based on three criteria:

1. Do you have obsessions—repetitive and persistent thoughts, images, or impulses that you experience as intrusive and inappropriate and that have caused significant anxiety or distress? A mental health professional will also want to know whether you try to resist these obsessions in some way. Furthermore, he will want to establish that you know that these thoughts and images come from your own mind and that you don't believe that someone or something has inserted these thoughts or images into your mind.

2. Do you have compulsions—repetitive behaviors or mental acts (mental compulsions) that you feel driven to perform in response to an obsession or according to certain rules? In particular, a mental health professional will want to establish that the sole objective of these behaviors or mental acts is to prevent or decrease the distress you experience or to prevent some feared consequence. She will also want to establish that you see that these behaviors and mental acts are both excessive and senseless.

3. Do these obsessions and compulsions significantly interfere with your day-to-day functioning—that is, do they take up a lot of your time or get in the way of important work, school, or personal activities? For example, if your compulsions take up more than one hour a day, on the average, then this may be excessive, even if the compulsions are brief but you do them frequently.

In addition, a mental health professional will rule out that the obsessions and compulsions are due to some other problem, such as a medical condition, drugs, or alcohol, or that another mental health condition better explains what you are experiencing.

Finally, a mental health professional will want to know whether you recognize, most of the time, that the obsessions and compulsions are excessive or unreasonable. The better your insight about your obsessions and compulsions, the more likely you are to benefit from treatment for your OCD.

THE EVALUATION PROCESS

The evaluation process has two broad goals: to confirm or disconfirm a diagnosis of OCD and, if the diagnosis is OCD, to collect information in order to develop a specific plan to treat it.

A comprehensive and detailed interview is the heart of the diagnostic process. The interview may take several hours, over several meetings. Through careful questioning, the mental health professional identifies whether you have the essential features, as described earlier, of OCD. In addition, she distinguishes between OCD and those other psychological conditions with which it is commonly confused. In addition, many people have other psychological conditions in addition to OCD, and other psychological conditions you might have can influence the treatment plan for your OCD. For example, most people with OCD are also depressed or, if not currently depressed, likely have had episodes of depression in the past. Someone who is significantly depressed may find it difficult to engage fully in the treatment for OCD. If this is the case, it might make sense to treat the depression first before beginning the treatment of the OCD.

With a diagnosis of OCD, a mental health professional can begin to collect information needed to develop a treatment plan. This is particularly important if your treatment is to include cognitive behavioral therapy (CBT). I will say more about CBT, which is the psychological treatment of choice for OCD, in chapter 3 ("Find the Right Treatment"). As part of the evaluation, the mental health professional asks about the content of your obsessions and whether the obsessions are thoughts, images, impulses, or some combination. The professional asks you to describe the objects or situations that trigger your obsessions and how uncomfortable you feel when these things trigger your obsessions. He will then want to know about the particular ways you try to get rid of obsessions (mental or physical) and the particular consequence or disaster you fear will happen otherwise.

The mental health professional asks many questions about compulsions too. She will ask you about the particular details of your compulsions and about how strong the urge is to engage in them. She asks how long it takes to carry out the compulsions;

how often you try to resist; whether the compulsions rely on set patterns, numbers, or sequences; and what happens if someone or something interrupts the compulsions. In addition, she will ask about the feared consequence—what you believe will happen if you don't do the compulsion.

TESTING

Mental health professionals make the diagnosis of OCD largely through interview. Most people will not receive formal psychological testing as part of the evaluation process. However, the mental health professional may ask you to complete a number of paper-and-pencil measures, such as questionnaires, checklists, or inventories (e.g., the Obsessive-Compulsive Inventory, the Compulsive-Activity Checklist, or the Yale-Brown Obsessive-Compulsive Scale). These measures list typical obsessive-compulsive symptoms and ask you to indicate which ones you struggle with now and have struggled with in the past. Often, these measures give a sense of not only your particular symptoms but also the severity of your OCD.

However, many people with OCD, particularly those who are perfectionists, have a great deal of difficulty completing measures like these. If the process of completing the measures is distressing you too much, or you are spending too much time trying to answer the questions "absolutely correctly," contact the mental health professional and let her know. You and she may be able to work out a plan to help you with the process.

Another important feature of the evaluation process is identifying other conditions or problems that may influence your response to treatment of your OCD. For example, the mental health professional may ask you to complete a measure of depression, such as the Beck Depression Inventory, or screen you for attention deficit/hyperactivity disorder (ADHD). Often, people with OCD are depressed or have long-standing problems with attention. If it is difficult for you to sit still or focus on what the mental health professional is saying to you, because you either are severely depressed or have ADHD, he may recommend treatment of these conditions before treating the OCD or at the same time.

There are no laboratory tests for OCD as there would be for a medical disorder such as anemia. Therefore, your mental health professional will not recommend laboratory tests unless he wishes to rule out a medical condition that may cause or influence some of your obsessive-compulsive symptoms. For example, people with thyroid disease may experience symptoms like those of OCD. A physician can detect thyroid disease with blood tests, and it is a good idea to ask your physician to run these tests, as well as others, to rule out conditions that can mimic anxiety disorders such as OCD.

SUMMING UP

As daunting as the evaluation process may sound, it's an essential part of your recovery from OCD. However, it's understandable if you are feeling a little nervous. You may worry about how the mental health professional will react to your symptoms because you may never have told anyone the full story. However, a professional who asks the right questions in a straightforward and caring manner may reassure you a great deal that you are not weird, immoral, or disgusting because you have certain obsessions and compulsions —you just have OCD. To that end, try to answer all the questions directly and honestly. The more information you can give the mental health professional about your particular symptoms, the more likely it is you'll receive an appropriate diagnosis. And just because you go to the evaluation doesn't mean you are signing up for treatment. The purpose of an evaluation or consultation is to gather information, and this goes both ways. It is important that you get answers to your questions too, in particular to find out whether you have OCD or not and if you do, what can be done to help. (For more on the questions you should ask, see chapter 4.)

In the next chapter, I describe the benefits of seeking treatment for your OCD at this time. If you decide now is the time, I describe the two most effective treatments for OCD—cognitive behavioral therapy and medication—as well as experimental treatments and other options available should conventional treatments not provide sufficient relief.

CHAPTER 3

FIND THE RIGHT TREATMENT

At first, I thought there was something wrong with my bladder or kidneys. I had to go to the bathroom and pee anytime I was going to do something important or enjoyable, even if I had peed just a few minutes before. I had to pee before I watched a movie on television or before I sat down to read the newspaper. I had to pee before I ate a meal or even made a telephone call. I just knew that if I didn't pee, I wouldn't be able to concentrate or even enjoy myself. After a while, I couldn't think about anything else. That's when I knew it was time to get some help.

—James

Fortunately, we don't need to understand what causes OCD to treat the condition effectively. Today, knowledgeable mental health professionals can successfully treat most people with OCD. In this chapter, I describe treatments that we know are effective in treating OCD, those we know won't help, and those that may help if conventional treatments aren't working.

TO TREAT OR NOT TO TREAT

If you have OCD, the thought of seeking treatment may fill you with added terror. You may worry that treatment will just make things worse or that the mental health professional may confirm your worst fear—that you are truly crazy or repugnant. However, as you will learn in this chapter, there are reasons to feel hopeful that things can get better for you.

While feeling anxious about treatment is understandable, there are dangers to doing nothing about your OCD. First, for most people, OCD tends to worsen over time, and symptoms that are somewhat manageable now are likely to become more intense and difficult to manage without help. As your symptoms worsen, you may become depressed, which adds to your suffering and the difficulty you can have getting through each day. Without treatment, people sometimes fall into unhealthy patterns of coping, such as using alcohol and drugs to lessen their anxiety. Without treatment, you may begin to avoid more and more activities and situations and pull away from friends and family members who could provide you with much-needed emotional support. As your

OCD worsens, the symptoms may further strain your personal relationships, which may cause your marriage or other important relationships to falter or fail. Without treatment, you may find it more and more difficult to do your job or even show up for work. Most important, however, is that your OCD may be robbing you of important opportunities for personal growth and happiness.

The primary downside to seeking treatment is that you must face your fears and distress as well as tolerate the feelings you may have when you admit to yourself and others that you have OCD.

COGNITIVE BEHAVIORAL THERAPY (CBT) OR EXPOSURE WITH RESPONSE PREVENTION (ERP)

The first-line psychological treatment for OCD is *cognitive behavioral therapy* (CBT). CBT combines two treatment approaches—*behavior therapy* and *cognitive therapy*. Behavior therapy assumes that we all learn to fear things, and the goal of this treatment is to help people learn not to fear things that are objectively safe. Cognitive therapy helps people change the irrational beliefs that contribute to fear of objects or situations that are objectively safe.

Exposure with response prevention (E/RP, or sometimes EX/RP) or *exposure with ritual prevention*, ERP) is a type of CBT used to treat OCD. Numerous studies from around the world have shown this to be an effective treatment for OCD, particularly for those with mild to moderate symptoms. ERP is particularly effective for those with contamination obsessions and washing compulsions and for those with excessive checking compulsions. For mild cases of OCD, treatment may take from four to eight sessions. Moderate cases typically require twelve to fifteen sessions, whereas severe cases may need more intensive and extensive ERP.

ERP begins with a careful assessment. You and your therapist decide which symptoms you will work on first, and the therapist will ask you to monitor the situations that trigger your obsessions and compulsions, how you respond (with compulsion, avoidance, or other strategies), and how anxious or distressed you feel. With this information, you and the therapist develop a hierarchy—a list of triggers that you rank on a scale of 0 to 100 (where 100 equals "severe anxiety or discomfort"). The therapist may ask you to rate your compulsive urges in the same way and to rate the intensity of the contamination feeling, particularly before and after exposures. The ERP hierarchy you developed with the therapist guides your treatment. The hierarchy spells out what exposures you will do and in what order, as well as where to start the ERP work.

Next, you and your therapist decide where on the hierarchy to begin. Your therapist asks you to trigger your obsession (this is the "exposure" part of ERP) while she is present and then sit with your discomfort instead of washing, checking, or doing anything else to lessen your anxiety or prevent the bad thing from happening (this is the "response prevention"). Typically, the therapist will show you what to do first or model the desired action for you. For example, if you are afraid of dirt or germs and you avoid touching door handles or the floor, the therapist might ask you to touch these things (after the therapist does it first) and then not wash your hands. The therapist will stay with you and from time to time will ask you to rate your level of anxiety or distress on the 0 to 100 scale. During these ERP sessions, your anxiety will rise but will also come down considerably so that near the end of the ERP session, your anxiety or compulsive urges are at least 50 percent lower than when you started the exposure. Initial ERP sessions may last two hours; as you progress, the therapist may shorten your sessions to one hour. In addition, your therapist will ask you to practice ERP tasks at home, perhaps with the assistance of a friend or family member who serves as your ERP coach (described in chapter 5).

COGNITIVE TREATMENT FOR OBSESSIVE THOUGHTS

Although ERP has been very successful in treating people with washing and checking compulsions, it has been less helpful for those who suffer primarily from obsessions without associated overt compulsions. Consequently, clinicians developed cognitive therapy as a complement to behavior therapy. As mentioned above, cognitive therapy helps people dispute the faulty thought patterns and irrational beliefs that result in obsessions. For example, images that she might molest her two-month-old child while bathing him or changing his diaper tormented a new mother. She assumed that these images meant she was, at worst, a pedophile or, at best, a horrible mother. She began to avoid any contact with her young son, which increased her belief that she was a horrible mother. In addition, as she tried to suppress these images, she had more of them, which further convinced her that she was about to molest her son at any moment. Cognitive therapy focused on helping her see the role her interpretations about normal intrusive thoughts played in the distress she experienced, which helped her better tolerate the unwanted and uncontrollable thoughts, which lessened her anxiety and the frequency of the obsessions themselves.

OTHER PSYCHOLOGICAL TREATMENTS

Over the years, mental health professionals have suggested that a number of other psychological treatments are effective for OCD. Most of the time, however, there is little or no evidence that these treatments work for OCD.

For example, research has not supported the effectiveness of most *traditional talk therapy*, particularly those forms based on *psychoanalytic* or *psychodynamic* theories. These theories assume that obsessions and compulsions are attempts by the person to keep unacceptable and anxiety-provoking memories, desires, and conflicts out of awareness. There is no evidence that psychoanalysis or psychodynamic therapy is effective for OCD.

There is no credible evidence that *hypnosis* is an effective treatment for OCD. During hypnosis, you receive suggestions that you will no longer have obsessions or that they will not trouble you and that you will be able to resist the compulsive urges you have. Although this approach sounds easier, in some ways, than CBT/ERP, there is no evidence that this approach significantly lessens OCD symptoms.

Eye movement desensitization and reprocessing (EMDR) therapy includes a number of strategies found in CBT but also includes a unique strategy: the therapist asks the client to hold in his mind an image of a distressing event while simultaneously tracking the therapist's finger as the therapist moves it back and forth across the client's visual field. EMDR appears to be as effective a treatment for post-traumatic stress disorder (PTSD) as other commonly accepted therapies, such as cognitive behavioral therapy. However, there is little strong credible evidence that EMDR is an effective treatment for OCD.

Acceptance and commitment therapy (ACT) appears to be a promising psychological treatment for anxiety disorders. The central tenet of ACT is that anxiety is part of life and it is our *reaction* to the experience of anxiety, rather than the anxiety itself, that creates problems for us. Practitioners have applied ACT to OCD with an emphasis on building mental flexibility rather than trying to eliminate distressing thoughts such as obsessions. ACT uses exposure techniques, like CBT, but within a different framework. Although there are few randomized controlled trials of ACT for OCD, most practitioners of ACT are familiar with CBT and understand the importance of exposure and response prevention in OCD treatment, and these appear to be central ingredients in ACT. However, it is not clear that ACT is more effective than CBT or that there are clear advantages to ACT over CBT/ERP.

For these reasons, CBT/ERP remains the psychological treatment of choice for OCD at this time.

MEDICATION TREATMENTS

Clinicians prescribe a variety of medications for OCD. In this next section, I describe the first-line medications for OCD, followed by typical *augmenting agents*—medication used to enhance the response to these first-line medications.

First-Line Medication

The first-line medication treatment for OCD is a course of a specific type of antidepressant medications. Now you might ask, "How can an antidepressant medication help me? I have OCD. I'm not depressed." Psychiatrists prescribe antidepressant medications for both anxiety disorders (such as OCD) and depression. In addition, many people with OCD are also depressed, sometimes severely. If that's your situation, you might consider trying antidepressant medication first before beginning CBT/ERP for your OCD. For some people, once depression is adequately treated, obsessions and compulsions disappear and don't require additional treatment.

You may be familiar with the class of antidepressant medications called *serotonin reuptake inhibitors* (SSRIs), which includes Prozac (fluoxetine), Luvox (fluvoxamine), Zoloft (sertraline), Paxil (paroxetine), Celexa (citalopram), and Lexapro (escitalopram). Although these medications are quite safe, they can have unpleasant side effects, such as nausea, insomnia, sweating, and headaches. However, most people tolerate these medications pretty well. Although some people with OCD respond well to lower doses, most people require a higher dose than they would for the treatment of depression alone and typically respond near the high end of the dose range.

Anafranil (clomipramine) is a *tricyclic antidepressant* medication, an older class of antidepressant medication, that is effective for OCD. Clomipramine appears to be as effective as SSRI medications in the treatment of OCD (Zohar and Judge 1996) and, for that reason, there may not be sufficient benefit to warrant the unpleasant side effects (particularly the dry mouth, constipation, drowsiness, and weight gain) of this medication over an SSRI. However, if you don't respond to the SSRIs, clomipramine may be worth a try.

Although some people respond very well to an SSRI medication, the average response is a 20 to 40 percent decrease in OCD symptoms, which is modest at best (Greist et al. 1995). Furthermore, if your OCD symptoms are mild, medications may not be necessary at all, and you may benefit from CBT/ERP alone. It appears that the SSRIs all work to about the same degree. Therefore, the prescriber may recommend one SSRI over another largely based on the particular side effects you may experience, the prescriber's experience with SSRIs, and whether your insurance company will pay for a particular SSRI.

The process of finding the right SSRI medication frustrates many people. Typically, it takes four to eight weeks before you and the prescriber know whether you will respond to a particular SSRI. If you don't respond, the prescriber will likely switch you to another medication and you will wait again to see if you respond. This waiting and switching can take many months. Furthermore, people who don't respond fully to one SSRI are likely to respond only partially to the next one they try as well.

Augmenting Medication

Although the SSRIs are effective medications for most people with OCD, some don't respond adequately to these medications, leading researchers to explore the use of other medication to augment or enhance the SSRI medication for those who don't respond well to an SSRI alone. *Neuroleptic* medications, also called *antipsychotics*, are the only augmenting agent shown to be consistently effective in decreasing OCD symptoms (Skapinakis, Papatheodorou, and Mavreas 2007). There are two kinds of antipsychotics. *Typical antipsychotics* have been around longer, but clinicians prescribe these less often now because of a serious side effect called tardive dyskinesia, which involves involuntary and uncontrollable movements of different parts of the body. Tardive dyskinesia is sometimes permanent if not caught early. Most often, clinicians these days will use an *atypical antipsychotic* medication, such as Risperdal (rispiridone), Zyprexa (olanzapine), and Seroquel (quetiapine), as an augmenting medication. These medications have less risk of tardive dyskinesia but can create metabolic problems that result in weight gain and elevated blood sugars and cholesterol. However, if taken under the careful supervision of a psychiatrist, these medications rarely cause long-term serious problems and, along with an SSRI, significantly decrease your OCD symptoms. Given the potential side effects of these medications, however, you will want to discuss thoroughly with your doctor whether the potential benefits of adding an atypical antipsychotic medication to the SSRI outweigh the risks.

Deciding Whether to Take Medication

Deciding whether to take medication for your OCD is a personal decision based on a careful discussion of the pros and cons with someone who is knowledgeable and experienced in prescribing medications to treat OCD. Medications don't help everyone, but we know that most people with OCD experience some improvement. There are particular times when medication might make sense for you; here are some examples:

- If you are severely depressed, starting your treatment with a medication might be the right thing to do.

- If you have other conditions, such as ADHD, a medication for that condition can help you focus and make better use of your CBT/ERP sessions.

- If the prospect of CBT/ERP for your OCD seems too scary and overwhelming, and you are finding it hard to make that first call to a qualified cognitive behavioral therapist, medications might help you take this first important step.

- If you are participating in CBT/ERP for your OCD and it doesn't appear to be helping, or your progress is too slow, medications might help you along.

- If you are feeling frustrated because you feel like you take one step forward and two steps back in your CBT/ERP, medications may help you make consistent progress on decreasing your symptoms.

- If you are finding that the exposures are too difficult no matter how small, medications might be worth a try too.

- If you cannot find a cognitive behavioral therapist in your community experienced in treating OCD, medications might be a good place to start as you continue to search for a qualified cognitive behavioral therapist to help you.

As you have learned, although most people tolerate OCD medications fairly well, medications do have side effects, and some of them are quite uncomfortable. The presence and extent of these side effects are likely the primary disadvantage of OCD medications for most people. However, some people with OCD refuse medications because of the OCD itself. For example, many people with OCD worry excessively about even the smallest side effect and tend to stop the medication before they achieve much benefit. People with contamination obsessions may not be comfortable taking any medications and often refuse to try an OCD medication. Many people with OCD are prone to indecisiveness and therefore have a great deal of trouble deciding whether to try medications. The default for indecisiveness is always inaction and, for that reason, people who have this difficulty postpone taking medication for their OCD for months or years. Last, some people with OCD refuse medications because they fear it means that they are weird, crazy, or weak. These fears are neither true nor good reasons to rule out something that might help you. In fact, once the medication begins to help, you will likely see things quite differently.

OTHER TREATMENTS

Unfortunately, not everyone with OCD who receives CBT/ERP and/or medications improves. In fact, some people's OCD is quite resistant to conventional treatments and, if symptoms are severe, these people might consider the following alternative treatments. However, bear in mind that these treatments, as you will read, are more drastic than those already described and are only for those who have not benefited from CBT/ERP and/or medications and continue to suffer greatly.

Brain Surgery

Most experts view brain surgery (or *psychosurgery*) as a treatment of last resort for chronic and treatment-resistant OCD. Clinicians originally used brain surgery to treat schizophrenia, and then they applied the procedure to other conditions, such as OCD. In brain surgery, the surgeon drills a hole in the skull and removes or destroys small amounts of tissue in specific areas of the brain. A newer form of brain surgery, *gamma knife surgery*, doesn't require opening the skull the way other brain surgeries do.

In this procedure, the surgeon focuses an intense beam of gamma rays that destroy tissue in a specific area of the brain. About 25 to 30 percent of those who don't respond to CBT/ERP or medications for OCD benefited from brain surgery (Schruers et al. 2005). Although these techniques are much more refined and have fewer side effects than in the early days, they are still an invasive and drastic form of treatment for OCD.

Electroconvulsive Therapy (ECT)

In *electroconvulsive therapy* (ECT), the clinician applies electrodes to the person's head and directs a weak electric current through the brain to induce convulsions. Prior to the treatment, the medical team anesthetizes the person and administers a muscle relaxant. Today, ECT has greatly improved. It is painless, and the person receiving it doesn't retain any memory of the procedure. However, there is no evidence that ECT directly improves OCD, unless the person is also depressed. ECT may therefore be an option for someone who has not benefited from CBT/ERP and/or multiple trials of medications but who still has severe symptoms of OCD and is deeply depressed.

Deep Brain Stimulation (DBS) Therapy

Since the mid-1980s, clinicians have used *deep brain stimulation* (DBS) therapy to treat movement disorders, such as Parkinson's disease. A surgeon implants electrodes in specific areas of the brain and then connects the electrodes with wires to a pulse generator that the surgeon implants under the skin (usually just below the collarbone). The implantable neurostimulator contains a microchip to control the stimulation and a battery to power the device. These devices are similar to a pacemaker, but the electrodes are in the brain rather than in the heart. Once the medical team has implanted the device, a doctor uses a handheld wand and a computer to set the pulse of the generator.

Using DBS to treat OCD is still an experimental treatment, although the FDA has recently approved DBS for treatment-resistant OCD under a Humanitarian Device Exemption that approves its use on a small number of patients. There are few clinical trials studying the effectiveness of DBS for treatment-resistant OCD; however, the studies that have been done suggest that DBS may provide hope for some people who have not responded to conventional treatments (Greenberg and Rezai 2003). There are two advantages to DBS over brain surgery. First, although implanting the electrodes does involve opening the skull, DBS doesn't require that the surgeon destroy any brain tissue. Second, DBS provides the medical team with a wider range of treatment because the doctor can adjust the intensity of the stimulation. However, to benefit from DBS, the person must continue the stimulation indefinitely.

SUMMING UP

We have treatments for OCD that help most people in a relatively short time. If your OCD symptoms are mild, you are likely to benefit from just CBT/ERP. If your OCD symptoms are moderate to severe, you may find a combination of CBT/ERP and medications is the right option for you. Although deciding to begin treatment is not an easy decision, there are many good reasons to begin now. The next chapter describes how to make certain you have found a professional knowledgeable in the treatment of OCD and how to get the most out of every therapy session once you begin.

CHAPTER 4

PUT TOGETHER YOUR TREATMENT TEAM

Now that I got the right help, it's hard to believe some of the crazy stuff I was doing. I used to believe that anything bad that happened was my fault. If I heard about a murder in the neighborhood, I thought that maybe I had done it. If I read about a car hitting some kid, then I worried that maybe I had hit the kid and didn't know it. I'd tell myself over and over, "I did not do it," but it didn't help. It got really crazy when I started to think that maybe I had murdered some kid in a state 3,000 miles away and I would check my credit card receipts to see whether I had bought plane tickets. I'd ask my friends when they last saw me or wrote notes with the date and time to reassure myself that I was here and not on the East Coast at the time something bad happened.

—Luke

Now that you know something about the right treatment for your OCD, it's time to put together your *treatment team*, which likely will include a psychiatrist or other medical professional qualified to prescribe medications and a cognitive behavioral therapist. This step is perhaps the most important and the most challenging for someone with OCD, because you are likely to bring some of the same anxiety, doubts, and difficulty with uncertainty to this process that you bring to your OCD. I will tell you right now—you will not find the perfect person to help you nor will you enter treatment without any doubts or unanswered questions. Although it's important that you feel confident in your treatment team and plan, it isn't necessary that you be completely confident. You may have some false starts, but it's important to begin immediately to seek help so that you can get on the road to recovery.

In this chapter, I walk you through the process of putting together your treatment team. The chapter begins with the process of finding the right therapist and prescriber and then moves on to explain how to get the most out of your therapy sessions. The chapter also describes the ins and outs of paying for your OCD treatment.

HOW TO FIND THE RIGHT THERAPIST

A *therapist* is a mental health professional trained to provide you with psychological rather than pharmacological (medication-oriented) treatment. Therapists include psychologists, social workers, mental health counselors, and marriage and family therapists. The state in which the professional practices licenses him, and he may or may not have much training in CBT for OCD. A *psychiatrist* can provide both psychological and pharmacological treatment. Regardless of title or license, you want to see a professional who has the appropriate training in the most effective OCD treatment—CBT/ERP.

It's important to feel comfortable with the mental health professional with whom you might work and also to feel confident that she understands OCD and is competent to treat it. During the evaluation process, your therapist probably asked you many questions, and some might have been tough questions, too. Now it's your turn to ask questions. Don't shy away from asking the tough questions that will help you decide whether this professional has the knowledge and skills to treat your OCD effectively. Following are the questions to ask any potential treatment provider.

What Specific Training Have You Received to Treat OCD?

Typically, it takes more than a workshop or class to learn CBT/ERP, the psychological treatment of choice for OCD. Mental health professionals who received training in special university clinics for OCD or anxiety disorders are likely to have received adequate supervised training in CBT/ERP for OCD. At times, mental health professionals will seek intensive training in CBT/ERP for OCD through the International Obsessive-Compulsive Foundation or through universities where many of the effective treatments for OCD developed, such as the Center for Treatment and Study of Anxiety at the University of Pennsylvania in Philadelphia. Typically, these intensive trainings include ongoing supervision for a period by experts in the treatment of OCD. Ask the professional whether he received this kind of training and, if he has, ask him to tell you a little about the training and the types of OCD cases for which he has received training and supervision.

How Many Cases of OCD Have You Treated?

Ideally, you are looking for an OCD expert—that is, someone who not only received adequate and appropriate training in CBT/ERP but also has treated more than a few cases. A true expert might evaluate and/or treat twenty or thirty people with OCD in a year, perhaps more if he practices in a specialty clinic or within a large urban center. Although it's not necessary that the professional treat a large number of people with OCD each year, you do want someone who has treated more than just a couple of people over the last several years. Again, you may not be able to find someone with this level of experience in your community, but asking about the number of cases treated can help you compare the professionals with whom you speak.

What Techniques Do You Use to Treat OCD?

If you are seeking treatment for the first time, it is essential that you receive the treatment known to be most likely to help you. That's CBT/ERP. Ask the mental health professional to tell you a little about how she goes about treating OCD. If she is vague or does not mention CBT/ERP, you can assume that she has not received much training in the treatment of OCD. Listen to the description for key CBT/ERP terms, such as "hierarchy" and "exposure." Feel free to ask the mental health professional what "response prevention" means or how she might conduct exposure with your particular symptoms. A professional experienced in treating OCD will be able to answer your questions directly and give you many examples to illustrate how she would apply CBT/ERP with you. If the answers to your specific questions are vague, or the professional suggests a treatment approach other than CBT/ERP or medications, you may want to consult with someone else.

What's Your Opinion about Medicine for OCD?

An experienced mental health professional will not only be open to medications but also be able to describe to you why it might make sense to include (or not include) medication in your treatment plan. If the professional is negative about medication or categorically refuses to consider medication as an option for you, this suggests the professional may not be a good fit for you given that medications are an effective treatment for OCD.

Are You Willing to Leave Your Office to Treat My OCD?

Many times, the best treatment of certain OCD symptoms happens outside the office. For example, if your OCD symptoms make it difficult for you to stay at work or to live comfortably in your home, you want a professional who is willing to accompany you into these situations to do CBT/ERP. Many mental health professionals are not comfortable providing treatment outside the office. However, most cognitive behavioral therapists do this all the time. They might drive with someone who is afraid to drive over bridges or, in the case of someone with OCD, help the person touch the doorknob of a public restroom without compulsively washing afterward. Although not everyone with OCD requires out-of-office CBT/ERP, if it makes sense for your particular OCD symptoms, you want a professional who will leave his office to help you.

In conclusion, to lessen your anxiety and doubts about the treatment process, it is essential that you are not only comfortable with the professional but also confident that she is qualified to treat your OCD. Asking these questions can help, as can doing your homework before the consultation appointment.

Remember—this is an important first step. You want to feel confident that you have the right plan and the right people to help you.

WHERE TO FIND THE RIGHT THERAPIST

In some areas of the United States, it is very difficult to find a qualified mental health professional in the community, much less someone with specific training and expertise in CBT/ERP for OCD. Nevertheless, you don't want to begin treatment with someone who will not provide you with the treatments known to help. It may be worth the drive to see someone outside your community if that person has the expertise you need.

Perhaps the best way to find a qualified cognitive behavioral therapist is to check several websites dedicated to providing accurate information to people with anxiety disorders (including OCD). The International OCD Foundation (ocfoundation.org) and the Anxiety Disorders Association of America (adaa.org) are two excellent sources for finding cognitive behavioral therapists experienced in treating OCD. In addition, the professional organizations to which a mental health professional belongs can tell you something about that professional's interests and expertise. For example, mental health professionals who are members of the Association for Behavioral and Cognitive Therapies (abct.org) or the Academy of Cognitive Therapy (academyofct.org) likely have expertise in cognitive behavioral therapy for anxiety disorders such as OCD. The Resources section at the end of the book · provides other ideas for finding qualified mental health professionals.

PRESCRIBERS

Mental health professionals licensed to prescribe medications for your OCD include psychiatrists, nurse practitioners, and some psychiatric nurses (with advanced training). In addition, your primary care physician can prescribe medications for your OCD. However, many primary care doctors prefer that you see a specialist, such as a psychiatrist, for help with medications, and there are advantages to receiving OCD medications from a psychiatrist rather than a primary care doctor. First, your primary care doctor must know hundreds of medications for many health problems, whereas a psychiatrist knows far fewer medications but understands them very well. Second, your primary care doctor is very busy and may not have the time to do as thorough an evaluation as a psychiatrist would provide. Last, because your primary care doctor is so busy, it might be difficult to schedule routine followup appointments after you begin the medication. These followup appointments are very important, particularly when you start a new medication or as you increase the dose. Remember, although these medications are safe for most people, they are powerful and do have side effects. A psychiatrist has the most training with and knowledge of the particular medications typically prescribed for OCD.

GETTING THE MOST OUT OF YOUR SESSIONS

Some people find CBT/ERP to be very demanding. It's true, facing your fears and going toward what makes you uncomfortable is no picnic. However, we know that CBT/ERP works—very well for some people—and that your fear and discomfort will decrease fairly soon with each new exposure. Nonetheless, if you are going to put yourself through this discomfort as well as invest considerable time and money in treatment, you want to make certain you get the most out of every session. Here are a few tips that will help.

Don't Withhold Information That Might Help

Some people don't tell their therapists about all the obsessions that trouble them. Perhaps they are ashamed that they have these thoughts, or they fear that the therapist will think they are crazy or disgusting. Some people don't tell their therapists about certain situations that trigger their obsessions and compulsions because they are afraid that the therapist will ask that they work on them. The tendency to withhold or conceal this kind of information is, as you have learned, one of the factors that maintains your OCD and, as importantly, prevents you from getting full benefit from your treatment. Even if you didn't tell the therapist the entire story at the consultation or even during the first few sessions of your treatment, you can share it at any time. Your therapist will appreciate just how difficult it is for you to share all the details of your OCD and will likely thank you for providing important information she can use to help you. Remember—you are learning to face your fears and tolerate your discomfort. Sharing information that is upsetting to you means you are working hard on your OCD.

Don't Try to Fly under the Radar

Some people will try to fly under the radar during exposure and perform minor compulsions rather than the full compulsion. They think that a minor compulsion can't do much harm. However, any ritual or compulsion, no matter how small, gets in the way of your getting full benefit from an exposure. If you are doing these stealth compulsions, tell your therapist. If you haven't yet done them but you're looking for ways to fly under the radar, tell your therapist that too. Perhaps he can modify the exposure so that you can resist all compulsions, even these small ones. Remember, to get full benefit from CBT/ERP, you cannot do any compulsions or other neutralization strategies while you're doing an exposure.

Do the Homework Just the Way You Agreed

Perhaps the single most important factor that distinguishes those who are successful in treatment from those who are less successful is how often they do their out-of-session CBT/ERP homework. In addition to the in-session CBT/ERP that you will do with the help of your therapist, your therapist will ask you to repeat what you did in session when you get home. True exposure occurs over repeated practices, often over several days, so you are likely not to get the full benefit of an exposure during the hour or so you meet with your therapist. However, the more homework you do, the faster you will see your discomfort or fear drop. In addition, it is important that you do the homework just the way you and your therapist agreed you would do it. Don't make any changes to the homework until you speak to the therapist.

It's true that exposures can be a bit more difficult when you try them on your own. That's where an *exposure coach* can help. Speak to your therapist about this. She may encourage you to bring a family member or friend to a therapy session to discuss coaching and to train your coach in the best way to support you in carrying out exposure homework.

Ask Your Therapist to Do It First

This is a small thing, but it can help many people who are feeling a little stuck. If you are having trouble starting an exposure, ask the therapist to do it first. Cognitive behavioral therapists call this *modeling,* and experienced cognitive behavioral therapists will not wait for you to ask. They will likely do it first to show you that there is no reason to be afraid. By watching your therapist do something that frightens you, your fear may decrease a bit and you may be more willing to try it yourself. For example, if you are having trouble touching the bathroom floor as your therapist has asked you to do, ask him to do it first.

Tell Your Therapist about New Symptoms or New Stressors

To be of the most help to you, the therapist needs to know what's going on with you, including any new OCD symptoms as well as any increase in your general stress level. People with OCD experience the same stresses as everyone else. They lose jobs, their marriages dissolve, and their children move away. These events can add stress to your life that then may cause your OCD symptoms to worsen. It's not likely the therapist will be able to decrease your OCD symptoms significantly if an ongoing stressor keeps making your symptoms worse. But if you inform the therapist about new stressors, she may be able to help you develop a plan to help. In addition, tell the therapist if the treatment is not helping you. Please don't worry about upsetting or disappointing her. If the current plan isn't working for you, it's better to get that out on the table so that you and your therapist can develop a better plan, such as adding a medication.

PAYING FOR TREATMENT

Now that you have put together the right treatment team, it's time to figure out how to pay for it. Many people don't have any insurance. Others have insurance, but it doesn't cover mental health treatment. Still others have insurance that covers mental health treatment, but the coverage they have doesn't cover nearly enough of the costs of quality mental health treatment; most health plans limit how much they will pay for each visit as well as the total number of treatment sessions you can have. Many health insurance plans require higher deductibles or copayments for mental health services than for other health services, and they often set lower limits on what they will pay per year or over your lifetime.

In 1996, the United States Congress passed the Mental Health Parity Act to equalize the way health insurance companies cover physical and mental illnesses. However, the legislation contains many loopholes, including the option for group health plans to exclude mental health benefits altogether. In addition, the law doesn't apply to health plans for companies of less than fifty-one workers, nor does it apply to health insurance that you purchase on your own. In 2008, legislators attached new mental health parity legislation to the economic recovery plan, but limitations still exist. Contact your state's insurance department to find out whether your particular health insurance covers payment for mental health services, and if so, to what extent.

Other than private insurance, the other way to pay for treatment is through Medicare or Medicaid. These are public insurance programs—paid for by federal and state governments—intended to provide health and mental health care to low-income individuals who meet eligibility criteria. However, most middle-class families don't qualify for these programs. For information about Medicaid eligibility, visit the Centers for Medicare and Medicaid Services website (www.cms.gov).

If you do have mental health coverage through either Medicaid or your employer, you likely will deal with a *managed care organization*. These organizations are set up to control or manage the costs of health care, including mental health care, and they take several forms:

- A *health maintenance organization* (HMO) has its own staff provide mental health services, although some HMOs contract with outside mental health professionals. If an HMO manages your health services, you must see one of their mental health professionals and likely must get a referral from your primary care doctor first.

- A *preferred provider organization* (PPO) is a managed care organization that gives you more choice over your mental health treatment. You may choose a mental health professional from their network of mental health professionals, and often you don't require a referral from your primary care doctor. You can call the PPO directly for names of mental health professionals in your community.

- The last type of managed care plan is *point of service* (POS), which gives you the most say in your treatment. As with a PPO, you can see a mental health professional within their network or you can seek treatment from mental health professionals outside the network. However, you likely must pay a higher copayment or deductible than with an HMO or a PPO.

If you have the resources, you can pay for your treatment yourself. Fees for psychotherapy or *pharmacotherapy* (treatment by medication) vary from state to state and even from community to community. In addition, psychiatrists may charge more than psychologists, who may charge more for the same treatment than a social worker or counselor. Many mental health professionals set aside one or two slots in their schedule for those who cannot pay the full fee. Ask the professional you've found whether he operates this way or has a *sliding scale*—that is, if he adjusts his fee downward for those with limited resources. In addition, you may find cost-sensitive treatment through universities or professional psychology schools in your area. In these cases, you may receive treatment from a student who is less experienced and knowledgeable but supervised by a licensed and more experienced mental health professional.

SUMMING UP

There are effective treatments for OCD, and most people can benefit from CBT/ERP, medications, or a combination of the two. In this chapter, you have learned how to go about finding the right professionals to help you and how to work with your treatment team. In addition, you have learned how to get the most out of every treatment session and something about paying for the treatments that can help you. The next chapter describes how to find the right support and how to seek appropriate support from friends and family members who are willing to help you.

CHAPTER 5

―――――――――――――――――――――――――――――――

FIND THE RIGHT SUPPORT

I hit bottom when my wife left me. She was fed up with my cleaning. I pretty much spent every moment—when I wasn't working, eating, or sleeping—cleaning the house. I washed the car every day when I got home from work. Even when the car had been in the garage all day, I washed it. I couldn't stand it if it had a speck of dust on it. I had to flush all the toilets when I got home, too, otherwise it didn't feel right, and sometimes I'd have to flush every toilet several times. I spent thirty or forty minutes every morning picking little bits of paper or leaves off the front and back lawn, otherwise I worried I'd feel uncomfortable all day long. You might think that a cleaning-crazy husband is a wife's dream, but she just couldn't take it anymore, and I don't blame her.

—Patrick

Appropriate support is an essential piece of your plan to recover from OCD. Support can take many forms, but the best support assists your recovery rather than undermines it. In this chapter, I describe the benefits of face-to-face support groups for you and your family members. I also describe the benefits of online support as well as the precautions you may want to take when seeking it. Then I take up the important topic of seeking appropriate support from friends, family, and your spouse or partner. Seeking support from loved ones can be a bit of a tightrope to walk for many OCD sufferers because OCD affects their family members too.

FACE-TO-FACE SUPPORT GROUPS

Self-help or *support groups* can be an important part of your treatment plan. Meeting with a group of people who have OCD can lessen the shame, isolation, and concealment that intensify your OCD symptoms. In addition to support, these groups offer information and resources, such as where in the community to find cognitive behavioral therapists experienced in treating OCD. If you are on the fence about whether to seek treatment for your OCD, a support group can be very helpful. Often someone who has benefited from CBT/ERP will sing its praises and help you see that things can be different for you. With the support and encouragement of group members, you may find it easier to take that first important step toward seeking evaluation and treatment for your OCD.

There are also support groups that can be helpful for your family members; groups provide them with a place to speak without fear or judgment, to vent if they need to, and to listen to others do the same. Many family members tell me how their participation in family support groups has improved their relationship with their loved one. In addition, as they listen to the stories told by other family members, they feel more hopeful that they can find some way to help too.

ONLINE SUPPORT GROUPS

Today, a growing number of people seek information from blogs and websites and support through online chat rooms. For some people, this form of support is ideal. For example, online support might be a good option if you have a medical problem that makes it difficult for you to leave your home or if you live in a remote area. If you are struggling about whether to make your OCD public, you might find that the anonymity of an online support group helps you take the first step toward overcoming the shame, embarrassment, and fear that may be holding you back from seeking help. However, online support groups are not for everyone and, in addition to the usual cautions about participating in online chat rooms, there are special considerations for those with OCD who are seeking this form of support:

- *Although online support is helpful, it is not a substitute for face-to-face support.* If you are socially isolated, online support may help you feel a bit more connected to others, but it is essential that you seek face-to-face help too.

- *Use appropriate caution when sharing information online.* Remember that you are sharing very personal information and that e-mail, blog entries, and inter-actions within a chat room are permanent (information that is stored on a computer somewhere may stay there for a very long time).

- *Try not to confuse seeking support with seeking reassurance.* If you are participating in online support groups or chat rooms or are scanning the Internet for information to help you feel less anxious about a particular OCD symptom, you may be making things worse for yourself. Although you are seeking reassurance to lessen the uncertainty that makes you anxious, at some point you will hear or read something that only adds to the uncertainty you are trying to eliminate through reassurance seeking, and you will feel more anxious and tormented by new doubts.

- *Confirm any information you gather or opinions you receive with a knowledgeable mental health professional.* There is a great deal of useful information online, and there is a lot of misinformation too. Don't assume what you read or what someone shares with you is correct.

- *Perhaps the best source of online support and information is through well-established nonprofit organizations.* Organizations such as the International OCD Foundation (ocfoundation.org) or the Anxiety

Disorders Association of America (adaa.org) have scientific advisory boards that include recognized experts on anxiety disorders in general and OCD in particular. For that reason, the websites of these organizations are more likely to have the most up-to-date and accurate information on the topic of OCD.

- *Remember that no two people with OCD are the same.* Although you may meet someone online with whom you share many similar symptoms, this does not mean that their situation is the same as yours or that their solution will be right for you. You're unique, and your situation is unique too. Take any advice you receive with a grain of salt.

SEEKING SUPPORT FROM FAMILY AND FRIENDS

Perhaps the most common reason family members give in to the OCD and reassure you when you are anxious, or do a ritual for you when you ask them to, is that they care about you and want you to feel better. For that reason, family members and friends can be important partners in your recovery. However, seeking support from your family, friends, or partner is not always straightforward. OCD has taken a toll on these relationships, and many people with OCD don't know how to begin the important task of seeking support from people who may have suffered by being close to someone who struggles with OCD. In this section, I describe how to talk to these important people about your OCD (or whether to tell them at all) as well as how to seek appropriate support for your recovery from the people who care about you.

Spouse/Partner

Seeking the support of your spouse or partner makes good sense for a couple of reasons. First, your OCD is "up close and personal" for your partner. She may be the one who has seen you suffer the most and likely has suffered a great deal herself. For that reason, she may be very motivated to find the right help for you and to support your recovery. Second, your partner has likely observed your symptoms in full bloom. You may not have held back at home in the way you have at work, at school, with friends, and even with other family members. Your partner likely knows the full extent of your OCD and your suffering and, for that reason, she can be a wonderful source of support.

The first step in seeking support from your spouse or partner is to share your recent diagnosis of OCD. Many times this is easy because he may have thought that you had OCD before you did. In fact, he may have been the one who first raised the possibility that you had it. This is often the case; someone who has lived with OCD all his life may just assume that everyone operates the way he does.

However, if your partner is as new to the OCD diagnosis as you are, sit down with her and explain that you finally know what has been going on with you. You may want to share this book or other resources you have gathered. Since OCD symptoms can be so different from person to person, you may want to give your partner only the descriptions of OCD symptoms that most closely match your own.

You may want to invite your partner to attend a few meetings with your therapist. Ask your therapist first, but most cognitive behavioral therapists will see the benefit of a few meetings with you and your partner focused on helping your partner participate appropriately in your recovery. If your therapist thinks that you and your partner would benefit from more assistance, she may recommend individual therapy for your partner or couples therapy with another therapist. Many times, couples struggle with the aftermath of OCD long after the OCD symptoms have lessened. For example, many couples harbor lingering resentments that they don't know how to talk with each other about. A couples therapist can help you discuss these past hurts and resentments and help you find ways that each of you can forgive the other. In addition, many relationships become so consumed with the OCD that a couple no longer remembers how to interact in a healthy way. Other times, partners spend more time doing things without each other because of the resentment caused by OCD or because they just want a break from the OCD symptoms. Once you have decreased your OCD symptoms through treatment, you may want to reengage with your partner and do things that you once enjoyed doing together. Your therapist or a couples therapist may be able to help you and your partner with this too.

However, there are times when it is not appropriate for you to share your diagnosis with your partner. At times, people with OCD have partners who are unreasonable and unsupportive, and no amount of apologizing or making amends changes the difficult nature of the relationship. A partner may refuse to participate in any way in your recovery. In fact, you may sometimes wonder if she is actively trying to thwart your attempts to get better. If that is the case, you might consider discussing with your therapist whether or not it makes sense to share your diagnosis with your partner. Your therapist might recommend that you and your partner seek couples therapy to work out some of the long-standing problems that may, or may not, be due to your OCD. Unfortunately, an unsupportive partner means you carry a heavier burden for your recovery, but you can still seek support from your therapist, friends, and other family members. If your mind is set on it, a supportive partner is not necessary for your full recovery from OCD.

Family

Your family can be a great source of support during your recovery from OCD. However, some of your family members may have suffered, as you have, from this difficult condition. For that reason and perhaps others, some family members may be better sources of support than others. In this section, I describe some general guidelines for seeking support from family members. But since every situation is unique, you may want to discuss with your therapist or a trusted friend the advantages and disadvantages of seeking support from specific members of your family.

In general, the family members who are the best sources of support are those who have the time, willingness, and ability to support you. Although your recovery is your responsibility, you or your therapist may ask family members to participate in certain ways. For example, you may want a family member to accompany you to your medication management meetings. At times, you may find it difficult to focus on or remember what your psychiatrist has told you because you have trouble concentrating due to depression, anxiety, or ADHD. Having a family member there to jot down notes or to check in with later can save you another call to your psychiatrist to double-check that you correctly remembered what he told you. With your permission, your therapist may want to ask a family member to coach you during out-of-session CBT/ERP practice. If you agree, the therapist will likely want to meet with you and your CBT/ERP coach to go over how best to support your exposures and what to do if you are having a hard time. Similarly, your therapist may ask your permission to contact this family member for updates on how often you are doing your CBT/ERP practice and how well you are resisting urges to engage in compulsions. The right CBT/ERP coach can make a big difference in how quickly you make progress in your treatment.

Certain family members who have the time and willingness to help you may be unable to support you for other reasons. For example, you may have a family member who is anxious or has OCD herself and is therefore not a good candidate for coaching you during CBT/ERP practice. However, this same family member may be able to accompany you to medication management meetings or even chauffeur you to your therapy sessions. You may have another family member who has serious health problems and doesn't have the energy to support your recovery, even though she wants to. However, this same family member could call you to praise your work and to remind you that things will get better if you keep your recovery on track.

Seeking support begins with sharing your diagnosis and, as described in the section on spouses and partners, some family members may be more helpful and welcoming of this first step than others. For the reasons I have described previously, sharing your diagnosis with the right family member can be enormously helpful.

You might ask, "Does sharing my diagnosis with family members include telling my children about my OCD?" Many parents with OCD struggle with this decision. You might wonder how it can help to tell your child that you have a mental health issue. Often, telling your children about your OCD can be very helpful to you and to them. For instance, children, like adults, can misinterpret what they observe. They might think you are fragile and may not tell you things about their personal lives because they worry you might become too distressed or upset. It is difficult to be an effective parent if your children are holding back about the problems in their lives, worrying that it will be too much for you. In fact, children might worry less about you when they know you have something called "OCD," particularly if you describe the condition in a straightforward and unemotional manner. Similarly, sharing your diagnosis may free your children to share their own worries and fears. We know that OCD runs in families, so one of your children may suffer with OCD symptoms too. Your courageous act of sharing your diagnosis and seeking treatment destigmatizes mental illness for your child and models the importance of seeking help when you are suffering.

Again, your therapist will help you decide whether it makes sense to share with your child or children that you have OCD. You may decide, for various reasons, that it makes sense to share with one of your children and not with another. For the child you decide to tell, there are several guidelines you may wish to follow. First, consider the age of your child when deciding what to share about OCD. For young children, a simple "I have OCD, and that's why I wash my hands so much" is enough. If your child is an adolescent, you can explain more about OCD and even offer articles or books to read about the condition and its treatment. Avoid sharing specific content about sexual or aggressive obsessions. It's okay to say only, "Sometimes I have very upsetting thoughts that make it hard for me to be around people." You needn't go into further detail, even if your child is older. Last, if your child is young, you may wish to reassure him that it isn't his fault, that you are getting help for your OCD, and that things will improve very soon. Encourage your child to come to you anytime with questions and, again, answer your child's questions with information that is appropriate to her age and with no more detail than is necessary to answer her specific question.

Friends

If you don't have family members (or if you do but they have never been a good source of support), you may have developed a solid group of friends who would be a wonderful source of support in your recovery from OCD. Even if your family is a good source of support, your friends can play an important role in your recovery too. However, friends may not know the full extent of your OCD because they see less of you than your family members do, or they may be completely unaware that you have OCD because you have successfully hidden your symptoms from them most of the time.

Just like spouses, partners, and family members, some friends will likely be better sources of support than others. You may want to discuss this with your therapist, and the two of you can look at the advantages versus the disadvantages of telling your friends at all, as well as which friends to tell if you decide to go ahead. However, even after careful consideration, you may share your diagnosis with a friend only to discover he is neither supportive nor welcoming of the news. At times, the news that you have OCD surprises a friend. He has one view of you and you are giving him another. Often, as you continue to be your usual self, your friend will see that you're no different now, really—you just have OCD. If your friend asks you questions, try to answer them directly. The more comfortable you show him you are with your diagnosis, the more comfortable he will become with this new information.

SEEKING APPROPRIATE SUPPORT

Seeking appropriate support for your OCD recovery plan begins when you ask your family members and friends to support *you*, but not your OCD. This means that you ask them to help you tolerate your distress rather than to step in to try to relieve it. Learning to tolerate your anxiety, fear, and discomfort rather than searching for ways to escape or avoid it is the central feature of an effective recovery plan for OCD. In addition, it is an essential feature of a recovery attitude, which I take up in the next chapter.

Seeking appropriate support also includes seeking hope rather than help from your family members and friends. Often, people in treatment for their OCD lose track of the progress they are making and begin to wonder whether things will ever get better. They can become demoralized, and then their motivation wavers. At these times, your family members and friends can "remoralize" you and renew your faith that things will improve because they notice the progress you are making, even when you do not. Treatment for OCD is a marathon—not a sprint—and most people experience a significant decrease in their symptoms initially, and then progress levels off for a bit. Ask your family members and friends to remind you of the progress you are making and to praise you for the small and large steps you are taking to overcome your OCD.

Seeking appropriate support includes asking family members and friends to stop participating in your symptoms—for example, by asking them to stop reassuring you or to stop checking or cleaning things for you. Usually, working this out with your family members with the assistance of your therapist is the best approach. The therapist can help you decide whether it makes sense to ask your family to withdraw their participation in your OCD gradually or to stop their participation immediately. In addition, the therapist can help you and your family members come up with what to say that is neither blaming nor undermining of your recovery. For example, you might want your family members to say, "I'm sorry, I'm here to support you and not to support your OCD. I won't do that anymore," or "Your therapist has asked me not to do that because it really doesn't help you." Regardless of what you and your family agree is the right phrase, it is essential that all agree to do their share. Your family agrees to say only what the therapist has coached them to say. You agree to accept what they say without anger or resentment. As you and your family replace this pattern of seeking inappropriate support with one of accepting appropriate support, you may notice that your OCD symptoms lessen significantly in a few days or a week.

A final way to seek appropriate support is to ask your family and friends to support your efforts in therapy, but not to assume responsibility for your therapy. Put another way, it's your therapy, not theirs, so it's not their job to monitor whether you do your therapy homework, whether you attend your therapy sessions, or whether you take your medication. Seeking appropriate support means that you ask your family to step back so that you can practice taking full responsibility for your recovery yourself. In a sense, through therapy, you are learning to be your own therapist, and it is important that your family members and friends give you the room to learn and practice that attitude.

SUMMING UP

Support can take many forms, as you have learned, and can play an important role in your recovery from OCD. With the right kind of support, you will recover faster from your OCD and maintain your recovery longer. Furthermore, as you begin to move away from inappropriate support, you will notice that your relationships with family members and friends change for the better too. Seeking and accepting appropriate support pushes OCD out of your life to make room for more caring and kindness.

In the next chapter, I describe the importance of cultivating a recovery attitude. A recovery attitude is essential to getting the most out of your treatment now as well as managing your OCD on your own after treatment ends.

CHAPTER 6

DEVELOP A RECOVERY ATTITUDE

I was going around and around with my OCD—literally—I drove around and around the block checking that I hadn't accidentally hit someone with my car. I know it's crazy now, but I really believed that maybe I hit someone and didn't know it. It used to take me over an hour to drive to work, which is only ten minutes from my house. Now that I got the right kind of treatment, I'm better, but the OCD still tries to trick me sometimes, and I really want to go back and check, but I don't. I've learned that I can't give in to the OCD, not even if it's a little check that won't take more than a second. You give an inch and it takes a mile.

—Shana

In many endeavors, "success" is 90 percent attitude. This is true when it comes to recovering from your OCD. By reading this book, you are showing that you're already on the road to recovering from your OCD because you are open to learning about OCD and to accepting help to deal with it. Openness, acceptance, and a willingness to feel uncomfortable are central features of recovery from most problems, including OCD. In this chapter, you will learn the key features of a recovery attitude and its importance for the short- and long-term success of your recovery from OCD. A recovery attitude includes healthy habits too, such as adequate exercise and sleep, and appropriate nutrition. This chapter will describe these healthy habits and the role they play in helping you recover from your OCD.

A RECOVERY ATTITUDE IS ESSENTIAL FOR TREATMENT SUCCESS

The successful treatment of your OCD depends on your developing an attitude that is counterintuitive to the way you have been operating. Through treatment, you will learn the value of tolerating discomfort, sitting with uncertainty, taking risks, and accepting imperfection. This new attitude will free you from the dread and fear that has caused you to pull further and further away from living a full and meaningful life. This new attitude will open your world again.

A RECOVERY ATTITUDE IS ESSENTIAL FOR LONG-TERM SUCCESS

Even those who benefit greatly from treatment for their OCD will notice, over time, that their hard-won gains erode ever so slowly. This erosion, in large measure, is because your recovery attitude has eroded over time. You may find yourself saying, "I'll wash my hands quickly, just this one time," or "I know nothing bad will happen, but why take a chance?" As you give in a little to your OCD, you will notice that it becomes harder to resist giving in a little more. Your compulsive urges increase, and your will to resist wavers and then weakens. Before you know it, you're back where you started. The recovery attitude you developed through treatment helped you to recover from your OCD. That same attitude will help you to maintain your progress over the long term too.

FEATURES OF A RECOVERY ATTITUDE

An effective recovery attitude toward your OCD consists of several important features.

Accepting Uncertainty

People with OCD tend to hate uncertainty. They check the locks because they aren't certain they locked them, even though they checked them just a minute before. They wash their hands because they aren't certain they washed off the last trace of dirt or germs. They avoid starting something until they're certain they will have the time to do it right. In other words, they constantly search for ways to transform the land of "maybe" into the land of "for sure" because if they are certain about something, they will feel less anxious. However, certainty is a myth—a comforting myth, but a myth nonetheless. A recovery attitude accepts that certainty is not possible and that the desire for certainty creates more problems than it solves. Acceptance or tolerance of uncertainty is the heart of any plan to recover from OCD.

Accepting Imperfect Outcomes

Achieving perfection is another comforting myth that people with OCD strive to reach. They have great trouble accepting imperfect outcomes. They work and rework a task because they believe that they can achieve perfection and thereby avoid mistakes and feel better about themselves. They analyze the pros and cons of each decision repeatedly and think that, through careful analysis, they will find the perfect solution and thereby achieve the perfect outcome. Through the treatment of your OCD, you will learn that imperfect outcomes are good enough, and, in fact, not so bad. As you become more comfortable with imperfect outcomes, you will become more comfortable with imperfect decisions as well. Accepting imperfect outcomes will help you to become more effective in life, which is the true goal of recovery.

Accepting Imperfect Knowledge

People with OCD sometimes feel that they need to understand something completely and perfectly. They spend hours researching a subject or ruminating about the complexities or the meaning of life. They have great trouble accepting that complete knowledge about anything is neither possible nor necessary. Many times, the need for perfect knowledge or understanding is the primary barrier to seeking treatment for OCD. Some people might search websites day after day for more information about OCD and their particular symptoms. They might call one mental health professional after another and pepper each with question after question, hoping to find the professional who has complete knowledge about OCD and therefore will be the best person to help. Through treatment of your OCD, you will learn to accept the discomfort that comes with not understanding something fully or perfectly. Accepting imperfect knowledge will help you stop searching for and begin accepting help for your OCD.

Looking for Opportunities to Step into Discomfort

Willingness to approach discomfort, rather than to escape it through compulsions or avoiding certain situations and objects, is an essential feature of your recovery from OCD. Once you learn the value of this attitude, your symptoms are likely to decrease quickly through CBT/ERP. However, OCD is a chronic condition, and you are always at risk of slipping back into a pattern of using compulsions or avoidance to lessen your distress unless you actively look for opportunities to step into discomfort. When you look for opportunities to feel uncomfortable, you turn OCD on its head. No longer are you searching for quick ways to escape your discomfort. Instead, you are looking for little ways to enhance your discomfort, such as running your fingers along a dusty windowsill or scanning the newspaper for an article on a topic that, in the past, you would have avoided reading. Viewing discomfort as an opportunity rather than a burden will help you manage your OCD over the years.

Turning Away from Debate

As you have learned in this book, compulsions are not the only way you might try to escape discomfort. You may find yourself trying to decrease your discomfort or prevent bad things from happening by engaging in relentless and endless debate with yourself. This, of course, all happens in your head, but debating with your OCD is just another way that you keep the OCD ball rolling. To turn away from debate means that you actively resist the urge to analyze, reassure, or reason with yourself:

- You refuse to analyze and reanalyze your thoughts and actions (for example, to ask yourself, Is it okay to think that? Does this mean I'm a bad person?).

- You refuse to reason with yourself by repeatedly going over the reasons why you would never do such a thing, even though the reasons are quite rational and true.

- You refuse to reassure yourself that you locked the door—"I checked it. I know I checked it because this is the fourth time."

- You refuse to repeat rational phrases that you may have come up with yourself or heard from others trying to help—"This is my OCD. This is my OCD."

In other words, you turn away from the internal debate with your OCD because you know that debating with it means you are in it.

Seeking Support, Not Reassurance

Recovery from your OCD includes support but not reassurance. Through treatment, you will learn the difference between the two, as will those who care about you and want to help. *Seeking support* means asking others to support your recovery plan and attitude. *Seeking reassurance*, on the other hand, means asking others to help you escape anxiety or discomfort. Seeking reassurance may give you some quick relief, but it won't last. In a few hours or days, you might again ask others to reassure you. Support is essential to your recovery—reassurance is not. Furthermore, the people who support you rather than reassure you will know that they are giving you something that is sustainable and ultimately in your best interest.

Not Giving OCD an Inch

After treatment, you may notice that your resolve to resist your compulsions begins to waver. You may think, "What's a little hand wash? It's not like it was before. I'll only wash for a second." You've been down that road before. You know that if you give OCD an inch, it will take a mile. Resist the urge to waver here and there. Remember, nothing terrible happened when you stopped your compulsions during treatment; why should something terrible happen now?

Typically, OCD begins to make a comeback in small ways—a quick wash here; a quick check there; a quick bit of reassurance here and there. Resist the urge to feed your OCD, even a little. Your recovery depends on it.

Practicing Every Day

Finally, a recovery attitude includes practice—practice every day. Near the end of treatment for OCD, you will have developed and moved through an ERP hierarchy. Remember, an ERP hierarchy is a list of exposures you and your therapist created and ranked from those causing you the least discomfort to those causing you the most. This hierarchy guided your ERP work as you moved up, doing exposures that were more and more challenging (see the section on ERP in chapter 3). Practice the exposures in the hierarchy every day, particularly those situations at the top (at the highest anxiety level) of your hierarchy. At the end of treatment, it's likely you'll no longer find these exposures very distressing. However, over time, what was once easy may become a little more difficult. Practicing exposures from your hierarchy every day keeps you in shape and enhances your resiliency to anxiety and discomfort. It's like exercise—use it or lose it. To stay in shape, practice every day.

A RECOVERY ATTITUDE INCLUDES HEALTHY HABITS

When you have OCD, it's difficult to take care of yourself. After living with OCD month after month, you may notice that it becomes harder to eat well and get enough sleep. You may struggle to fit even a walk around the block into your schedule. After all, you have the same amount of time in a day as everyone else— twenty-four hours—but your OCD has started to take more and more time away from you. Something must give. You have to work, but perhaps you can cut back on exercise or sleep. Perhaps you can save a few minutes by eating some fast food on the go or by getting up earlier or staying up later to squeeze into each day what OCD demands from you and what life asks of you too. To benefit fully from treatment and to maintain your recovery over time, it is essential to have a recovery attitude that includes healthy habits as well.

Appropriate Exercise

Regular, vigorous exercise is one of the best stress- and mood-management strategies and an essential part of an effective recovery plan. Exercise costs little or nothing and reduces muscle tension, dampens arousal, and discharges pent-up frustration and anxiety.

You don't need much exercise to feel better—just thirty minutes a day, three times a week. If it's been difficult for you to begin and maintain a regular exercise routine, find yourself an exercise buddy. Ask a friend to join you for a walk in the morning or take walking breaks at work with a coworker or two. Now and then, you may be able to discuss business with a coworker during a walk rather than in your office. A good exercise buddy is someone who is at about the same ability and endurance level and who enjoys the kind of exercise you do. Knowing that you are meeting a friend or coworker for an exercise break can make the difference between getting out and staying in.

However, because you have OCD, it is important that you don't overdo. In particular, don't exercise just because you are feeling very anxious or because you are having a compulsive urge. It's a slippery slope between a healthy habit and an exercise compulsion for those with OCD.

Proper Nutrition

Proper nutrition is the cornerstone of a healthy body. In addition, proper nutrition can play an important role in your ability to manage your anxiety and OCD. Glucose is the fuel your body burns, and much of the glucose comes from the breakdown of complex carbohydrates in foods such as bread, potatoes, fruits, and vegetables. Your body converts these carbohydrates slowly to glucose, which keeps the level of glucose in your body at a consistent level over the course of the day. This steady level of fuel keeps your energy and mood up and makes it possible for you to do the many things you do throughout the day. Simple sugars, on the other hand, break down very quickly to glucose. Many processed foods you eat include simple sugars—foods such as refined white sugar, brown sugar, and honey. Because simple sugars break down so quickly, a high concentration of glucose enters your bloodstream suddenly, often overwhelming your body's ability to regulate its sugar level. This can lead to higher levels of anxiety or fluctuations in your mood. Although proper nutrition won't eliminate your OCD, it can put you in a better place to manage your OCD symptoms during the day.

Try to cut down on your consumption of refined sugars and processed foods. Eat more fruits and vegetables as well as grains, such as whole grain rice and cereals. Cut down on the amount of salt you use too. Excessive salt consumption can raise your blood pressure and deplete your potassium level; potassium helps your nervous system function properly.

Of all the foods that you eat or drink, those with caffeine can most directly influence your anxiety. Too much caffeine can keep you chronically tense, aroused, and on edge. Coffee, tea, cola beverages, chocolate, and some over-the-counter drugs have caffeine in them. Excessive caffeine consumption can even result in panic attacks. Because some people are more sensitive to caffeine than others are, you may want to try eliminating or greatly limiting your caffeine consumption for four or five months, just to see if it makes any difference in your stress level. You may be surprised just how much better you feel with just a single cup of coffee in the morning. If you are having sleep difficulties, you may want to eliminate caffeine altogether and try not to use it as a pick-me-up if you are fatigued.

Adequate Sleep

Adequate sleep is essential and goes a long way toward calming your mind and body. If you are not getting adequate sleep, you may find that you are more anxious in general and have less resilience to day-to-day stress. You may find it hard to focus at work or that you are more irritable and down if you don't get enough sleep. If you are tired, you may find it even more difficult to resist your compulsive urges or to participate fully in the treatment of your OCD.

Although how much sleep we all need changes over time, you know you are getting enough sleep when you awaken refreshed in the morning and remain alert throughout the day. If this is not the case, you may be able to get your sleep back on track by changing your sleep habits and environment.

Build a transition period into your bedtime routine. At least an hour before you go to bed, turn off the television and computer. The light from some screens sends a message to your brain to stay alert and awake, so it helps to give your brain a break from screens before bed. Switch to a relaxing, eyes-open activity, such as reading, knitting, or working on a jigsaw puzzle. These relaxing exercises send a signal to your brain that it's time to downshift toward sleep.

We have more control over when we get out of bed than when sleep comes, so try to get up at the same time every day, even on weekends. A regular sleep pattern will help to keep your sleep on track—and don't nap. Instead, when you are tired, stand up and stretch or go for a quick walk around your office or the block. This will help to snap your brain back into the alert mode.

The right environment can help sleep come more easily. Make certain your bedroom is quiet, dark, and cool. If your room is noisy, turn on a fan or use earplugs. Don't watch television or work in bed. Reserve your bed for sleep. If you do, when you lie down in bed, your brain will remember that sleep happens in bed and will begin to downshift.

Work-Life Balance

As you have learned, if you have OCD, you likely have an inflated sense of responsibility. This can cause you to take on more than your share of responsibility at work or at home. A sense of responsibility can make you a great employee or a busy homemaker, but an *inflated* sense of responsibility can make it tough for you to maintain an appropriate work-life balance. Over time, your OCD may cause your life to drift more and more out of balance. As your life becomes less balanced, you may find that you're more fatigued and therefore less efficient at work and home. In an effort to keep up, you may choose work over your personal life, which causes you to become more isolated from the support of family and friends. As you become more isolated, you are more and more alone with your OCD, which only makes your symptoms worse. Over time, you may begin to burn out and become depressed too, making it harder for you to do anything. However, there are ways to regain balance in your life.

Saying no can be difficult for anxious people and for those with OCD; saying no may cause them to feel unreasonably guilty too. However, it is essential that you *learn to say no* if you are to return balance to your life. When you say yes to your coworkers or boss, you are, in essence, teaching them to come to you rather than to other people in your office. They may have to work a little harder to get other people to say yes, but you're easy: you usually say yes. Once you say no a few times, you teach people to think twice before they come to you with something they would like you to do. Saying no takes practice but saying no will make more room in your life for family and fun.

With the internet, cell phones, and smart phones, work issues may easily intrude on your nonworking time and people can reach you 24/7, if you let them. To achieve work-life balance, you may have to *create a boundary between work and home* for yourself. Calendar personal activities the way you do work activities and resolve that once a personal activity is in your calendar, it is as important as a work activity. This will help you protect your time from the relentless drift toward work. Create an imaginary boundary on your commute home that signals you are entering personal time and space. For example, select a landmark along your route home from work, perhaps the steeple of a church, the marquee of a theater, or a billboard. Try to find something that you can see some distance away. Watch for this landmark on your commute home and, when you see it, use it to remind yourself that you have left your workspace and entered your personal space.

Build downtime into your schedule. Set up a regular date night with your partner or schedule Monday nights with friends or family to watch the ball game. If you don't get much alone time, get up thirty minutes earlier than the rest of your family so you have a little time to read the paper without interruption. The most important thing is to schedule downtime into your calendar to protect and prioritize it. Start small—just a few minutes of downtime here and there can make a big difference. Break away and walk to the cafeteria or restroom "the long way." That extra two minutes is yours.

SUMMING UP

In this chapter, you learned the importance of developing a recovery attitude in order to overcome your OCD now and to maintain your recovery over the long term. You also learned the essential features of a recovery attitude and that, by shifting your attitude, you can get the most out of your recovery. Last, you learned the important role healthy habits—such as exercise, nutrition, and sleep—play in your recovery, as well as a few things you can do to improve these habits in your life. In the next chapter, you will learn something about the unhealthy ways some people with OCD cope and what you can do if that is happening with you. You will also learn about other psychological issues that occur when someone has an anxiety disorder such as OCD.

CHAPTER 7

UNHEALTHY COPING AND OTHER PSYCHOLOGICAL ISSUES

It's funny how we slip into unhealthy patterns when we have OCD. Sure, there's the OCD pattern of anxiety and compulsions, but then there's the unhealthy pattern of drinking to cope with my OCD. The toughest thing in my recovery from OCD was letting go of the alcohol. Once I made the decision to change that, my recovery from the OCD went along much faster.

—Milton

Many people with OCD suffer with other psychological issues or cope in unhealthy ways. In addition to having OCD, chances are good that you are depressed or suffer with another anxiety disorder. You may have resorted to alcohol and drugs to try to get through the day or to get some relief at night from your anxiety and obsessions. You may have started to overuse your prescription medications for this purpose too, and your physician and family may have grown even more concerned for you.

In this chapter, you will learn about the unhealthy ways some people with OCD try to cope and what you can do if you are using substances in this way. You will also learn the other psychological issues or conditions with which you may struggle if you have OCD and what you can do to get help for these problems too.

UNHEALTHY WAYS OF COPING

If you have OCD, there is about a one in three chance that you have or have had a problem with alcohol or drugs at some point in your life (Mancebo et al. 2009). Although people with OCD are less likely to abuse alcohol or drugs than are people with other mental health problems, such as schizophrenia or bipolar disorder, about 15 percent of people with OCD have a serious substance abuse problem (Yaryura-Tobias et al. 1996).

Most people with OCD begin to use substances to lessen their anxiety and discomfort and to cope with the day-to-day consequences of living with OCD. People with OCD may use substances as a coping strategy, but over time this strategy creates more problems for them than it solves. If you abuse substances to lessen your anxiety, you may notice it works at first, but the next day you may feel more anxious or depressed. Over time, you may notice that it takes more alcohol or drugs to get the same relief. This can cause you to use more alcohol or drugs in a maddening effort to keep your OCD at bay. In addition, substance abuse can take a toll on your relationships, your work life, and your self-esteem; which, in turn, increases your stress and your desire to avoid dealing with your OCD and other problems.

Finally, using substances doesn't really treat your OCD; it reinforces avoidance, which, as you have learned, keeps the OCD ball rolling. Furthermore, if you are in treatment for OCD, either with medications or CBT/ERP, the substances will make it difficult for you to receive the full benefits of these treatments. In particular, alcohol and drugs can interfere with the exposure tasks that are central to CBT/ERP for OCD. CBT/ERP depends on your learning to tolerate discomfort and anxiety in the short term with the promise of feeling less anxious and uncomfortable in the long term. Substances get in the way of your learning this very important lesson.

Alcohol

If you have OCD, there is an 8 to 10 percent chance you abuse alcohol, and the younger you were when your OCD started, the more likely it is that you will abuse alcohol (Gentil et al. 2009). Chronic alcohol use can lead to serious medical problems, such as cirrhosis (liver damage), diabetes, and heart disease, and it can worsen your OCD over time. In addition, if you are depressed, repeated alcohol consumption can worsen your depression, thereby making it more difficult for you to function in your personal and work lives.

If you are taking medications for your OCD, or you are considering it, you must be particularly careful about your alcohol use. For example, if you are taking benzodiazepines, these medications interact with alcohol such that you may feel more sedated and more impaired than with alcohol alone. Similarly, if you are taking a medication for another psychological problem that co-occurs with your OCD, such as ADD, you must be careful about your alcohol use too. If you are taking stimulant medications for ADD, for example, you may not feel the usual effect of the alcohol until the medication wears off, but your reflexes may still be impaired. You will learn more about the consequences of prescription-drug abuse later in this chapter. Even if you don't have a substance abuse problem, it is wise to ask your doctor about potential side effects from consuming alcohol while on the medications for your OCD.

Nicotine

Despite our knowledge of the major health hazards of tobacco use, approximately 21 percent of the US population, or about forty-five million people, continue to smoke (Centers for Disease Control and Prevention 2000). The number of people with anxiety disorders who smoke is even higher (Lasser et al. 2000). Interestingly, people with OCD smoke less often than do people with other anxiety disorders, perhaps because they have other health-related fears or obsessive fears of germs or contamination (Morissette et al. 2007). However, if you do smoke and would like to quit, it is important to get some help because people with anxiety disorders tend to have a more difficult time quitting than other people (Breslau, Kilbey, and Andreski 1992). Speak to your doctor about your desire to stop smoking. Medications, such as Wellbutrin/Zyban (bupropion), Chantix (varenicline), and nicotine patches or gum can help ease the withdrawal symptoms, and psychological treatments can help too, particularly when combined with nicotine replacement therapy (Carmody et al. 2008; Evins et al. 2008).

Marijuana and Cocaine

Although some people with OCD report that marijuana calms the mind and lessens compulsive urges, at this time, there isn't any evidence that medical marijuana is an effective treatment for OCD. Although marijuana might provide some short-term relief from your OCD symptoms, it can lead to loss of motivation, short-term memory problems, and drowsiness. Furthermore, if you are depressed, marijuana can worsen your depression and lead you to withdraw more often from pleasant activities that help lift your mood.

Cocaine can cause you to feel agitated, paranoid, and aggressive. Furthermore, those who use cocaine are at greater risk of developing OCD than people who don't use cocaine and/or marijuana (Crum and Anthony 1993). If you abuse cocaine, you may abuse alcohol too, and this combination compounds the danger of either drug taken alone. Researchers have found that the human liver combines cocaine and alcohol to produce a third substance, cocaethylene, which is associated with a greater risk of sudden death than cocaine alone (Harris et al. 2003).

Prescription Medications

Many people believe that medications their doctor has prescribed for them are safe to take under any circumstances. This is not true. Prescription drugs act directly or indirectly on the same parts of the brain that illicit drugs affect. For that reason, people who use these drugs inappropriately face risks of addiction and adverse health effects similar to those who use illicit drugs. Furthermore, prescription drug abuse is growing at an alarming rate, particularly among adolescents and young adults. The most commonly abused prescription medications are pain relievers, tranquilizers, and stimulants. Pain relievers that contain opioids, such as OxyContin (oxycodone) and Vicodin (hydrocodone/ acetaminophen), act on the same brain receptors as heroin and therefore can be highly addictive. In addition, opioid-based pain relievers, alone or in combination with alcohol, can depress respiration and cause death. The number of fatal poisonings involving prescription pain medications has more than tripled since 1999 (National Institute on Drug Abuse 2010).

Doctors typically prescribe tranquilizers, such as Ativan (lorazepam), Xanax (alprazolam), or Klonopin (clonazepam), for severe anxiety or sleep problems. These tranquilizers depress the central nervous system and at high doses can cause respiratory depression and death, particularly when combined with alcohol. These medications are addictive and, especially for those who use them regularly at high doses and over long periods, can cause seizures or other life-threatening problems if you stop taking the medication or stop taking it too quickly. Furthermore, even when used as prescribed, these medications can interfere with exposure therapies such as CBT/ERP for your OCD because they interfere with your body's natural tendency to become comfortable, over time, in situations that currently make you anxious.

In a study of college students, about 8 percent use stimulant medication without a prescription (McCabe, Teter, and Boyd 2006). Stimulants, such as Adderall (mixed amphetamine salts immediate-release), are often prescribed for ADHD or narcolepsy and can lead to addiction and serious health consequences, such as seizures, cardiovascular problems, and psychosis.

It is essential that you take your medications only as prescribed and according to your doctor's specific instructions. If you have questions about your medications, check with your doctor first before increasing your dosage, stopping the medications, or changing the medication plan that you and your doctor worked out.

SIGNS YOU MIGHT HAVE A PROBLEM

Substance abuse can creep up on people, and sometimes it's difficult to know whether you have a problem with alcohol or drugs. Here are three warning signs that you might have a substance abuse problem:

- *Tolerance*—This is the first warning sign that you may have a problem. You are building a tolerance to a substance when you consume more and more of it to get the same effect. For example, you used to get a "buzz" from one glass of wine but now it takes two or three. Can you now smoke more marijuana than other people can without getting high? Do you take a drink or two before a party to get a head start because you know that you will need more alcohol than other people to feel the same effect? The amount of time it takes to develop a tolerance for a substance depends on the particular substance you use, the amount of it you use, and how often you use it.

- *Withdrawal*—This is how your body responds when you cut back or stop using a substance. Do you take a drink to steady the shakes in the morning? Do you smoke a joint to settle the nausea in your stomach or to feel less agitated or angry? Using a substance to relieve or avoid withdrawal symptoms is a huge warning sign that you have a problem.

- An *out-of-control life*—In addition to the two warning signs above, another sign that you may have a problem is that your life is slowly spinning out of control. Do you spend a lot of time thinking about how to get a substance and when you can next use it? Do you continue to use a substance even though you know it's causing problems? Do you want to quit drinking or using a substance, but you can't stop or even cut down? Have you given up important activities, such as spending time with family and friends, working out, or pursuing hobbies because you would rather use? If you answer yes to any of these questions, you may have a problem with substances.

GETTING HELP

If you think you might have an alcohol or drug problem, speak to your doctor or a mental health professional about your drug and alcohol use. Tell them directly about what, how much, and how often you use. If you have been abusing alcohol and drugs for a long time, it is essential that you speak to a physician before you stop cold turkey because of the possible withdrawal effects. In fact, some withdrawal effects, such as seizures, are dangerous, and your doctor or mental health professional might suggest a treatment program to help you safely stop your alcohol or drug use. Remember, it will be difficult for you to recover fully from your OCD as long as your alcohol or drug use is a problem.

OTHER PSYCHOLOGICAL ISSUES THAT OCCUR WITH OCD

People with OCD typically have other disorders or conditions, such as depression, other anxiety disorders, attention deficit disorder, and obsessive-compulsive spectrum disorders. During your evaluation, your mental health professional will screen for these and other psychological issues because, if they are not adequately treated, these can make it more difficult for you to recover from your OCD.

Depression

Depression is the most common problem for those with OCD (Crino and Andrews 1996; Steketee et al. 1999). Investigators estimate that as many half of those with OCD struggle with major depression or have experienced an episode of depression in their lifetime (Nestadt et al. 2001). Usually, people become depressed after the onset of their OCD and in response to the distress and impairment caused by their OCD symptoms. In addition, the more severe or distressing the obsessions or compulsions, the more likely it is that the person will become depressed in part because he begins to feel helpless and hopeless about the problem. On occasion, however, people can develop obsessions after they become depressed. Generally, the obsessions leave when the depression lifts.

Other Anxiety Disorders

People with OCD also tend to have additional anxiety problems (Weissman et al. 1994), in particular, social phobia, panic disorder, and generalized anxiety disorder.

Perhaps as many as a third of people with OCD have *social phobia* (Nestadt et al. 2001). People with social phobia worry excessively about what people might think of them. They worry that people think they are boring, unattractive, or weird and then they avoid certain social situations. If you have OCD and social phobia too, it may be even more difficult for you to seek treatment or continue treatment because of your excessive fears about how others, including your therapist, might view you. Social phobia can compound the shame and embarrassment people with OCD already feel about their particular obsessions and compulsions. CBT and medications are effective treatments for social phobia.

About 20 percent of people with OCD have *panic disorder* too (Nestadt et al. 2001). Panic disorder is an excessive fear and worry about having a panic attack in certain situations. Many people with OCD have had a panic attack when something triggered an obsession and their anxiety escalated quickly until they panicked. However, not everyone who has panic attacks worries about future panic attacks and therefore develops panic disorder.

Last, about one in ten people with OCD have *generalized anxiety disorder* (GAD), which is excessive and exaggerated worry about everyday things (Nestadt et al. 2001). If you have GAD, you might worry excessively about your job, your health, or world events. In fact, you likely are worrying about something most of the time, which may make it difficult for you to sleep or cause you to feel tense and keyed up all day long. Again, antidepressant medications and CBT are very effective treatments for panic disorder and GAD. If you have other anxiety disorders in addition to your OCD the treatment may be a bit more complicated. For that reason, it is important that your therapist be very experienced in CBT for OCD and other anxiety disorders.

Attention Deficit Disorder

People with OCD can have difficulties with concentration, attention, and processing information and, for that reason, may think they have *attention deficit disorder* (ADD). For example, if you are counting or praying to yourself or trying to keep a distressing image or thought out of your mind, you may appear to others to be inattentive, forgetful, or restless. In addition, some people with ADD will engage in what appear to be OCD behaviors to compensate for the ADD. If you have ADD, it's likely you have forgotten to lock a door or to put an important document in your backpack or briefcase. You compensate now by checking and perhaps rechecking, just in case. You might make lists because you know lists help to keep you on track, or you are rigid about always keeping your keys or your checkbook in the same place. This does not necessarily mean you have OCD. On the other hand, if you have OCD, there is a 25 percent chance you have ADD too (Masi et al. 2006), so it is very important that the mental health professional you see evaluates you separately for each disorder so that you receive the proper treatment. If you have ADD that is untreated, it might be difficult for you to get the full benefit from CBT/ERP for your OCD because you have trouble focusing during your sessions with the therapist or following through with out-of-office homework because you forget about it. If this is the case, speak to your therapist about medications for your ADD.

Obsessive-Compulsive Spectrum Disorders

Obsessive-compulsive spectrum disorders (OCSD) are now believed to be biologically linked. OCSD includes classic OCD, hypochondriasis, body dysmorphic disorder, eating disorders, Tourette syndrome, trichotillomania, and compulsive skin picking and nail biting.

Between 13 and 15 percent of people with OCD have hypochondriasis (Jaisoorya, Janardhan, and Srinath 2003; Nestadt et al. 2001). *Hypochondriasis* is the preoccupation with fears of having a serious disease, such as cancer. People with *body dysmorphic disorder* (BDD) are preoccupied with an imagined defect in appearance, such as "my nose is crooked." Although people may describe themselves as obsessed with their health or their looks, hypochondriasis and body dysmorphic disorder are not OCD. People with hypochondriasis are exclusively obsessed with their health and do not have other OCD symptoms (e.g., fears of contamination or aggression). People with BDD are exclusively obsessed with their appearance and report few other intrusive and distressing thoughts.

Perhaps as many as 10 percent of people with OCD have an eating disorder, such as bulimia nervosa or anorexia nervosa, and more often these are women (Sallet et al. 2010). When you have *bulimia*, you consume an abnormally large amount of food (*binge*) and then make yourself vomit, use laxatives, or exercise excessively to counter the feelings of disgust and anxiety you feel after the binge episode. When you have *anorexia*, you are terrified about gaining weight and severely limit your intake of food and calories such that you become dangerously underweight. Almost

37 percent of people with anorexia have OCD (Thornton and Russell 1997), which suggests that people with OCD may be more likely to develop anorexia than people who do not have OCD. If you think you may be bulimic or anorexic, tell your doctor or mental health professional so that you can get appropriate treatment for these life-threatening conditions.

About 3 to 5 percent of people with OCD have *Tourette syndrome*; however, about 68 percent of people with Tourette syndrome have some OCD symptoms (Rasmussen and Eisen 1990), and the considerable overlap between these two disorders suggests a genetic link (Green and Pitman 1991). Although people with OCD or Tourette syndrome engage in fixed and repeated movements, the tics in Tourette syndrome are spontaneous acts caused by a sensory urge. These motor acts or tics reduce sensory tension, but people with Tourette syndrome do not consciously tic to escape obsessive anxiety or discomfort. In contrast, people with OCD deliberately use compulsions to reduce fear or discomfort.

People with *trichotillomania* repeatedly pull out scalp hair, eyelashes, eyebrows, or other body hair. About 3 to 4 percent of people with OCD have trichotillomania (Nestadt et al. 2001). Although people with trichotillomania can feel guilty, ashamed, and anxious because of the chronic hair pulling, they do not have obsessions. Furthermore, when you pull your hair, you may experience some pleasurable feelings after the pull, whereas you feel little pleasure from checking or hand washing, only some relief from your obsessive anxiety or discomfort. Speak to your doctor or mental health professional if you think you might have Tourette syndrome or trichotillomania in addition to your OCD. We now have effective treatments for these conditions, which include medications and/or habit reversal training.

Compulsive skin picking or *nail biting* are similar to trichotillomania because these conditions also involve senseless, body-focused repetitive behaviors. Although people feel quite distressed by the consequences of the compulsive skin picking or nail biting, they experience both relief from tension and pleasurable feelings. Speak to your dermatologist, primary care doctor, or mental health professional if you think you might have a problem with compulsive skin picking or nail biting. Treatment for these problems is similar to the treatment for trichotillomania and includes medications and/or habit reversal training.

SUMMING UP

If you have OCD, you may be prone to using alcohol or drugs to cope or struggle with other psychological issues or conditions, such as depression, other anxiety disorders, ADD, and obsessive-compulsive spectrum disorders. In this chapter, you learned how these issues can influence your recovery from OCD and what to do if you think you might have one of these problems. In the final chapter, you will learn how OCD can affect your performance on the job or at school and what you can do if this is happening.

CHAPTER 8

WORKPLACE OR SCHOOL ISSUES

It got so I couldn't really do my job. I checked every e-mail six or seven times before I sent it; then I checked it that many times after I sent it. I'd write lists to help me remember and then lists of the lists. I had notes all over my computer, my door, my desk, just to help me check less, but the lists didn't really help. I checked all my work over and over until I was exhausted. I was working twelve hours or more a day, and at least three or four of those hours were OCD hours. I thought I was going to lose my job, and maybe I would have if I hadn't gotten some help.

—Jose

You may have sought help for your OCD because it was affecting your ability to do your job or to do well in school. OCD will do that, and many people find it more and more difficult to be effective in the workplace or school setting because of their OCD. In this chapter, you will learn the ways OCD can affect your performance on the job or at school. You will learn whether it makes sense to tell coworkers or your supervisor or your teachers that you have OCD and, if it does make sense, how to go about sharing this information. This chapter goes on to describe your rights in the workplace and in school and the kinds of accommodations that might make sense for you.

WHEN OCD STRIKES IN THE WORKPLACE

One of the reasons you may have sought help for your OCD is that it was affecting your ability on the job. OCD can strike at the workplace in several ways. It can affect your productivity if you are overly meticulous, perfectionistic, and need to have things "just so." This can lead to missing project deadlines or failing to complete projects at all. You may have trouble delegating work to others because you worry that they won't complete the work to your standards, which only leads to more stress and work for you and more missed deadlines. Similarly, because you are overresponsible, you take on too many projects, and this adds to your stress and workload. The stress, workload, and overresponsibility make your work so unpleasant—in fact, punishing—that you may procrastinate about starting that memo, e-mail, or the first step in a big project. The procrastination only adds to your stress, late nights, and job burnout.

OCD can affect the quality of your work too. People with OCD sometimes overfocus on the details of a project. This is the classic case of not seeing the forest for the trees. This can also lead to missing project deadlines or spending hours rewriting a memo to get the grammar just right or to make certain you didn't misspell a single word. In addition, you may find that the quality of your work suffers because you have trouble focusing or concentrating during the day. The difficulty you have focusing may be because you are depressed, anxious, or just working hard to push the unpleasant thoughts and images from your awareness.

OCD may affect your attendance too. You may frequently be late to work or to meetings because of your washing and checking rituals. Your OCD may make it difficult for you to work effectively with your colleagues because you have unreasonably high standards for yourself and them. Your coworkers or supervisor may become frustrated with your tendency to seek clarification about the simplest task or to seek repeated reassurances from them before you begin a project or even write an e-mail.

At the same time, a little OC can make you a responsible and hardworking employee. However, those with OCD don't always know when they have crossed the line that separates the dedicated and hardworking employee from the employee burdened with OCD. If you are working harder and harder to keep up with your work and falling further and further behind, you may be wondering whether it is time to tell your employer about your OCD.

Your Rights in the Workplace

The Americans with Disabilities Act (ADA) protects you from discrimination by an employer due to mental illness, such as OCD. In addition, a prospective employer cannot deny you employment simply because you have OCD, if you are otherwise qualified for the position. Although this is the law, many people with OCD have had quite different experiences when they told their employers that they have OCD. For that reason, it is important that you carefully consider the potential costs and benefits of telling or not telling your current or potential employer about your OCD and that you discuss this with your therapist, if you are currently in treatment.

According to the ADA, to have a qualified disability, you must have a record of or be regarded as having a substantial, as opposed to minor, impairment. In addition, if you have a disability, you must also be qualified to perform the essential functions or duties of the job, with reasonable accommodations. This means that, first, you must satisfy your employer's requirements for the job, and second, you must be able to perform on your own, or with the help of reasonable accommodation. A *reasonable accommodation* is any change or adjustment to a job or work environment that permits a qualified applicant or employee with a disability to participate in the job application process or to perform the essential functions of a job.

To Tell or Not to Tell

Whether or not to tell your employer about your OCD is a difficult decision and can be a very scary idea for many people. You may worry about how your boss will react to your diagnosis. Will she accept and help you, or will she reject and dismiss you as a complainer or troublemaker? You may worry that once your boss knows about your OCD, she will not promote you or will no longer trust you with important tasks or responsibilities. Worse yet, you may worry that your employer will fire you or blacklist you within your industry. You may worry about your coworkers' reactions too. On the other hand, it may be getting more and more difficult to do your job or even to get to work, so there are risks and benefits on both sides of the decision.

According to the ADA, it is generally the responsibility of the applicant or employee with a disability to inform an employer about the possibility of needing an accommodation. In other words, nothing happens until you tell the employer you have OCD, meaning that telling your prospective or current employer about your diagnosis is the only way to guarantee your right to the accommodations you may need to maintain employment. Nonetheless, you have no obligation to tell your prospective or current employer about your OCD.

If your OCD symptoms are mild and manageable, there may not be any benefit to telling your employer about your diagnosis. However, if your symptoms are severe and getting worse, you may find it hard to hide your OCD, and your employer (who may not know you have OCD) may raise these issues during performance evaluations. If that is the case, telling your employer about your diagnosis may protect you and set in motion a process whereby you can receive help that enables you to continue to work.

The decision to tell your employer or not may depend on how the employer has helped other employees in the past who have disclosed they have a mental health issue. Some employers do only what they must do under the law, whereas other employers go that extra mile to help an employee continue to work. Speak to coworkers or the Employee Assistance Program (EAP) representative, if you have one, about your company's record on helping its employees with disabilities. In addition, check your company's Human Resource department for written policies for employees with disabilities in the workplace. These policies are open to you and fully available for your review.

If your employer has an EAP, or has contracted with one, you might want to ask the EAP representative about the best way of telling your employer about your diagnosis. The EAP representative has likely done this before and can help you navigate this delicate process. If the employer doesn't have an EAP, you may need to tell your boss or supervisor yourself. Tell your boss only as much as he needs to know about your OCD in order to receive the accommodations that will help you. You may need to educate your employer if he doesn't know what OCD is or about the challenges people with OCD can have in the workplace.

Reasonable Accommodations in the Workplace

Accommodations are no substitute for proper treatment, and it can reassure and help set the right tone for seeking accommodations if you can tell your employer that you are receiving appropriate treatment for your OCD. Once you tell an employer about your diagnosis, the ADA requires your employer to provide reasonable accommodations, but, as with so many things, the devil is in the details. So you may want to think through exactly what kinds of accommodations might help you. Discuss these with your therapist and write them down together. Make certain they specifically describe what you need to function effectively in the workplace.

Reasonable accommodations for OCD in the workplace will depend on your particular symptoms, but typically, they include adjustments to your schedule or to workplace tasks. For example, if getting to work on time is a problem because of your OCD or appointments with your therapist, or if your medication causes drowsiness in the morning, you might ask for a flexible schedule that permits you to come in later in the morning and work later in the day.

You might ask your employer to shift responsibilities you have from one task to another. For example, if a certain task requires some counting or verification, ask for tasks that don't require (or require less) of this. If you tend to overfocus on the details of tasks, ask for a job coach through your state's vocational rehabilitation office who can help you focus on the bigger picture and encourage you to shift focus and check less. The job coach can also assess your workplace and identify areas where you may become stuck because of your OCD and then interface between you and the EAP or HR office to design a plan to help. At times, the job coach can work with your therapist to help you do ERP in your workplace if there are particular areas that are a problem.

If your OCD is so severe that you think or your employer thinks a leave of absence is necessary, consider the risks and benefits to you of this decision too. In general, it is better to work, when possible, than not to work. A leave of absence is a serious decision that has implications for your financial safety, self-esteem, and future employment. In addition, work also provides structure and distraction that can help you manage your symptoms, and the tasks of your job can limit the frequency of your compulsions and tendency to avoid. Discuss a possible leave of absence carefully with the EAP representative and your therapist to clarify the risks and benefits to you of a leave of absence.

WHEN OCD STRIKES IN SCHOOL

OCD is not, strictly speaking, a learning disability, but it can certainly affect how well you do in school. OCD strikes at school in much the same way it does in the workplace: You may have trouble getting to class on time. You may be losing sleep trying to keep up with the workload because it takes too long to read materials or to complete assignments. You may not be able to enter a classroom because you fear that the room or a classmate is contaminated.

In other words, OCD negatively affects your ability to get to classes, do the work, and work with other students and your teachers. Furthermore, if you have a roommate, the OCD may make it difficult to share a room if you feel that your room and space must be a certain way.

Your Rights in the Classroom

By law, every college or university in the United States must allow a student with a disability equal access to programs and services. In other words, the school cannot refuse you admission to college or into a particular class because you have OCD. In addition, the school must provide reasonable accommodations for you so that you can access the academics and other programs in the school setting. Furthermore, by law, the college or university must protect information about your OCD. For example, the school cannot include information about your diagnosis or any accommodations you received because of your OCD in your transcript or permanent record. Most colleges have a disabilities office for students. Sometimes this is within the Dean of Students office. The disabilities office is the place to seek information about the policies of your particular school regarding students with disabilities, such as those with OCD.

Reasonable Accommodations in School

By *accommodation*, I mean an adjustment to the curriculum or the classroom that will help you stay in school, access the curriculum, and generally get through the day. However, accommodations are not an effective long-term strategy for getting the most out of school and, without treatment, are not likely to be enough to help you succeed fully in school. Accommodations are there to help you get by until you get into treatment for OCD and your symptoms lessen.

To receive accommodations in a college or university, you must tell the school that you have OCD and provide documentation from a professional that verifies this diagnosis. Documentation of your diagnosis can come from your current psychiatrist or cognitive behavioral therapist or a mental health professional who has evaluated you in the past. In addition to your diagnosis, the documentation must explain how your OCD disability affects your functioning—in particular, your ability to learn, study, and take care of yourself in school. You may have received accommodations when you were in high school, for example, through a 504 plan or Individualized Education Program (IEP). However, accommodations you received in high school don't transfer automatically because different laws apply to high school and college. Your high school plan, however, may provide the college with a good place to begin when developing its own accommodation plan for you.

Typically, the plan you and your college work out for you will include *reasonable accommodations*. "Reasonable" is the key word here because the college may refuse you accommodations it considers unreasonable, such as changing an essential aspect of a course. For example, the school may not permit you to avoid using chemicals in a chemistry lab course because the use of chemicals is an essential aspect of the chemistry lab curriculum.

Typical accommodations can include permission to use your own paper and pencils if contamination obsessions make it difficult for you to use the test booklets provided by your teacher. The school may give you priority for classes that meet later in the morning if getting to school on time is a problem because checking compulsions make it difficult for you to arrive on time to classes. You may want to seek additional academic support too. The College Living Experience website (cleinc.net) provides information to students needing additional academic support because of mental health issues, such as OCD, or because of a learning disability.

If you are not in college but entering soon, you may want to contact the disabilities office at each college as part of your decision about which college is the best one for you. The disabilities office can provide you with helpful information about the kind of support they provide students with disabilities. In deciding which college to attend, you may also want to consider whether there are mental health professionals in the college community who are qualified to treat OCD.

Seeking Help on Campus

If you are struggling in school because of your OCD, the first step is to seek help. Most colleges have a student health center, clinic, or counseling service to assist students with their mental health needs. Your student health service may be able to provide you with medications and/or CBT, or they may refer you to a qualified mental health professional in the community. The Resources section at the end of this book can help you find appropriate mental health professionals near your school.

Although your school is perhaps the quickest and most cost-effective way to seek help, it has drawbacks too. If your college is small, you may see classmates or dorm mates when you walk in and out of the mental health clinic. Many times, your student health service will provide only a few sessions of treatment and then refer you to a mental health professional in the community, if you require more help. In addition, the counseling staff may not have the expertise to treat your OCD adequately and can offer only medications to you.

Taking a Medical Leave

It is always best to stay in school if you can, particularly if you are in treatment for OCD. The day-to-day structure and distractions of school can help you manage your OCD. If you are in treatment, it may help to stay in school to work on the things in your school environment that trigger your OCD, such as your dorm room, classrooms, roommates, cafeteria food, or bathrooms. However, if your OCD is so severe that you are concerned that your grades will really suffer or that you won't be able to make it through the quarter or semester, you might consider a medical leave of absence from college. However, taking a medical leave from school is a big decision with both benefits and costs to you.

If you decide to take a medical leave, remember that things could change when you return to school. You may have a new dorm room, new roommates, and different classes and teachers. If you have student loans, a scholarship, fellowship, or other financial assistance, there may be financial risks of taking a leave too. Speak to someone in the financial aid office before you take a leave, to see if your financial aid will continue when you return from a medical leave. In addition, if you decide to take a leave of absence, make certain that the school records the leave in order to extend the payback time of your loan.

During your leave, it is essential that you seek treatment for your OCD and use that time to focus on your recovery. If you're in therapy, discuss the decision with your therapist first. If you're not in therapy, seek therapy before you decide to leave college. You can discuss the costs and benefits of a medical leave and work out a plan with your therapist on the best way to do this, if you decide to go ahead with it.

CONCLUSION

In this book, you have learned about OCD and the ways it can make your life difficult, how to get the right diagnosis, and the treatment options (such as medications and CBT/ERP). You have learned how to put together a strong treatment team and to find other kinds of support that can help you in your recovery from OCD. You have also learned about the importance of a recovery attitude for succeeding in treatment now and maintaining your recovery in the future, the features of a recovery attitude, and the changes you can make in your personal health to better manage your OCD.

You've become aware of the unhealthy ways people with OCD sometimes try to cope and how to change if this is happening to you. You've also discovered the ways OCD can affect your workplace or school performance and what to do if that happens.

Given all that you have learned, don't forget the most important thing: With the right treatment and the right treatment team, most people with OCD get better, and some get very much better. Learning about your condition and accepting your diagnosis is the first—and perhaps the most important—step in your recovery. I wish you every success in your journey toward less fear and a fuller and more meaningful life.

Resources

BOOKS

Abramowitz, J. S. 2009. *Getting Over OCD: A 10-Step Workbook for Taking Back Your Life*. New York: Guilford Press.

Antony, M. M., and R. P. Swinson. 1998. *When Perfect Isn't Good Enough: Strategies for Coping with Perfectionism*. Oakland, CA: New Harbinger Publications.

Baer, L. 1991. *Getting Control: Overcoming Your Obsessions and Compulsions*. Boston: Little, Brown & Co.

Ciarrochi, J. W. 1995. *The Doubting Disease: Help for Scrupulosity and Religious Compulsions*. Mahwah, NJ: Paulist Press.

Colas, E. 1998. *Just Checking: Scenes from the Life of an Obsessive-Compulsive*. New York: Pocket Books.

Foa, E. B., and R. Wilson. 1991. *Stop Obsessing!* New York: Bantam Books.

Goodwin, S. 2003. *Colleges for Students with Learning Disabilities or ADD*. St. Louis, MO: San Val.

Hesser, T. S. 1998. *Kissing Doorknobs*. New York: Bantam Doubleday Dell Publishing.

Hyman, B. M., and T. DuFrene. 2008. *Coping with OCD*. Oakland, CA: New Harbinger Publications.

Hyman, B. M., and C. Pedrick. 2010. *The OCD Workbook*. 3rd ed. Oakland, CA: New Harbinger Publications.

Keuthen, N. 2001. *Help for Hair Pullers*. Oakland, CA: New Harbinger Publications.

Kravets, M. 2010. *K & W Guide to Colleges for Students with Learning Disabilities or Attention Deficit/Hyperactivity Disorder (ADHD)*. 10th ed. Framingham, MA: The Princeton Review.

Munford, P. R. 2004. *Overcoming Compulsive Checking*. Oakland, CA: New Harbinger Publications.

———. 2005. *Overcoming Compulsive Washing*. Oakland, CA: New Harbinger Publications.

Neziroglu, F., J. Bubrick, J. A. Yaryura-Tobias, and P. D. Perkins. 2004. *Overcoming Compulsive Hoarding*. Oakland, CA: New Harbinger Publications.

Osborn, I. 1998. *Tormenting Thoughts and Secret Rituals*. New York: Pantheon Books.

Pedrick, C., and L. Fitzgibbons. 2003. *Helping Your Child with OCD*. Oakland, CA: New Harbinger Publications.

Pedrick, C., K. J. Landsman, and K. M. Parrish. 2005. *Loving Someone with OCD*. Oakland, CA: New Harbinger Publications.

Phillips, K. A. 1996. *The Broken Mirror: Understanding and Treating Body Dysmorphic Disorder*. New York: Oxford University Press.

Purdon, C. 2005. *Overcoming Obsessive Thoughts*. Oakland, CA: New Harbinger Publications.

Rapoport, J. 1989. *The Boy Who Couldn't Stop Washing*. New York: Penguin Books.

Sisemore, T. A. 2010. *Free from OCD: A Workbook for Teens with Obsessive-Compulsive Disorder*. Oakland, CA: New Harbinger Publications.

Steketee, G., and K. White. 1990. *When Once Is Not Enough: Help for Obsessive Compulsives*. Oakland, CA: New Harbinger Publications.

Tolin, D. F., R. O Frost, and G. Steketee. 2007. *Buried in Treasures: Help for Compulsive Acquiring, Saving, and Hoarding*. New York: Oxford University Press.

Tompkins, M. A., and T. L. Hartl. 2009. *Digging Out: Helping Your Loved One Manage Clutter, Hoarding, and Compulsive Acquiring.* Oakland, CA: New Harbinger Publications.

Wilensky, A. 1999. *Passing for Normal—A Memoir of Compulsions.* New York: Random House.

TREATMENT CENTERS

Aldea Psychological Services
695 Central Avenue, Suite 106
St. Petersburg, FL 33701
Phone: (727) 331-9592
Website: aldeapsychologicalservices.com

Anxiety & Agoraphobia Treatment Center
112 Bala Avenue
Bala Cynwyd, PA 19004
Phone: (610) 667-6490
Website: www.aatcphila.com

Anxiety Disorders Center/Center for Cognitive Behavioral Therapy
The Institute of Living/Hartford Hospital
200 Retreat Avenue
Hartford, CT 06106
Phone: (860) 545-7390
Website: harthosp.org/instituteofliving
/anxietydisorderscenter/

Anxiety Disorders Treatment Center of Chapel Hill and Durham
421 Bennett Orchard Trail
Chapel Hill, NC 27516
Phone: (919) 942-0700
Website: anxieties.com

Anxiety Solutions of Northern New England
P.O. Box 70
Raymond, ME 04071-0070
Phone: (207) 655-2737
Website: anxietysolutions.net

Anxiety Treatment Center
8980 Alderson Avenue
Sacramento, CA 95826
Phone: (916) 366-0647
Website: anxietytreatmentexperts.com

Austin Center for the Treatment of Obsessive-Compulsive Disorder
6633 Highway 290 East, Suite 300
Austin, TX 78723
Phone: (512) 327-9494
Website: austinocd.com

Behavior Therapy Center of Greater Washington
11227 Lockwood Drive
Silver Spring, MD 20901
Phone: (301) 593-4040
Website: www.behaviortherapycenter.com

Bio Behavioral Institute
935 Northern Boulevard, Suite 102
Great Neck, NY 11021
Phone: (516) 487-7116
Website: biobehavioralinstitute.com

Center for Anxiety and Obsessive Compulsive Disorders
Alexian Brothers Behavioral Health Hospital
1650 Moon Lake Boulevard
Hoffman Estates, IL 60169
Phone: (847) 882-1600
Website: www.abbhh.org

Center for the Treatment and Study of Anxiety
University of Pennsylvania
3535 Market Street, 6th Floor
Philadelphia, PA 19104
Phone: (215) 746-3327
Website: anxietystudycenter.org

Center for Understanding and Treating Anxiety
San Diego State University
6386 Alvarado Court, Suite 301
San Diego, CA 92120
Phone: (619) 229-3740
Website: http://nas.psy.sdsu.edu

Cognitive Behavior Therapy Center for OCD and Anxiety
990 A Street, Suite 401
San Rafael, CA 94901
Phone: (415) 456-2463

Website: cbtmarin.com

Houston OCD Program
1401 Castle Court
Houston, TX 77006
Phone: (713) 526-5055
Website: www.houstonocdprogram.org

Kansas City Center for Anxiety Treatment
10555 Marty Street, Suite 100
Overland Park, Kansas 66212
Phone: (913) 649-8820
Website: kcanxiety.com

Lindner Center of HOPE
4075 Old Western Row Road
Mason, OH 45040
Phone: (513) 536-4673
Website: lindnercenterofhope.org

Mayo Clinic
200 First Street SW
Rochester, MN 55905
Phone: (507) 284-2511
Website: www.mayoclinic.org/obsessivecompulsive-rst/index.html

McLean Hospital Obsessive-Compulsive Disorders Institute
115 Mill Street
Belmont, MA 02478
Phone: (617) 855-3279
Website: mclean.harvard.edu/patient/adult/ocd.php

Mount Sinai Center of Excellence for OCD and Related Disorders
1425 Madison Avenue
Mount Sinai School of Medicine
Dept. of Psychiatry
Icahn Bldg., 4th Floor
New York, NY 10029
Phone: (212) 241-8177
Website: mssm.edu/research/centers/center-of-excellence-for-ocd

Obsessive-Compulsive Disorder Center and CBT Services
Rogers Memorial Hospital
34700 Valley Road
Oconomowoc, WI 53066
Phone: (262) 646-4411
Website: rogershospital.org/monroe/content/obsessive
-compulsive-disorder

Obsessive Compulsive Disorder (OCD) Research Clinic
Yale OCD Research Clinic
34 Park Street, 3rd Floor
New Haven, CT 06508
Phone: (203) 974-7523
Website: psychiatry.yale.edu/research/programs/clinical_people
/ocd.aspx

OCD and Anxiety Treatment Center
3030 Starkey Boulevard, Suite 128
New Port Richey, FL 34655
Phone: (727) 569-2239
Website: www.ocdandanxietytreatment.com

OCD Research Clinic at Butler Hospital and Brown University

345 Blackstone Boulevard
Providence, RI 02906
Phone: (401) 455-6214
Website: www.butler.org/ocd

OCD Resource Center of Florida

3475 Sheridan Street, Suite 310
Hollywood, FL 33021
Phone: (954) 962-6662
Website: ocdhope.com

Saint Louis Behavioral Medicine Institute

Anxiety Disorders Center
1129 Macklind Avenue
St. Louis, MO 63110
Phone: (314) 534-0200
Website: slbmi.com/anxiety_center/

UCLA Anxiety Disorders Program

300 UCLA Medical Plaza, (2nd Floor)
Los Angeles, CA 90024
Phone: (310) 206-5133
Website: www.semel.ucla.edu/adc/

University of Florida OCD Program

P.O. Box 100234
Gainesville, FL 32610
Phone: (352) 392-3611
Website: psychiatry.ufl.edu/Patient-Care-Services/OCD-Program/

University of North Carolina Anxiety and Stress Disorders Clinic

Department of Psychology
CB#3270, Davie Hall
Chapel Hill, NC 27599
Phone: (919) 843-8170
Website: psychologyclinic.unc.edu/anxiety

University of South Florida Rothman Center for Pediatric Neuropsychiatry

800 6th Street South
4th Floor North, Box 7523
St. Petersburg, FL, 33701
Phone: (727) 767-8230
Website: health.usf.edu/medicine/pediatrics/rothman/index.htm

Western Psychiatric Institute and Clinic

University of Pittsburgh Medical Center
3811 O'Hara Street
Pittsburgh, PA 15213
Phone: (877) 624-4100
Website: www.upmc.com/HospitalsFacilities/Hospitals/wpic/Pages
/DepressionAnxiety.aspx

Western Suffolk Psychological Services

755 New York Avenue, Suite 200
Huntington, NY 11743
Phone: (631) 351-1729
Website: wsps.info

Westwood Institute for Anxiety Disorders
921 Westwood Boulevard, Suite 223
Los Angeles, CA 90024
Phone: (323) 651-1199
Website: hope4ocd.com

ORGANIZATIONS

Academy of Cognitive Therapy
Website: academyofct.org
Email: info@academyofct.org
Phone: (267) 350-7683

American Psychiatric Association
Website: psych.org
Email: apa@psych.org
Phone: (888) 357-7924

American Psychological Association
Website: apa.org
Phone: (800) 374-2721

Americans with Disabilities Act
US Department of Justice
Website: www.ada.gov
Phone: (800) 514-0301

Anxiety Disorders Association of America
Website: adaa.org
Email: information@adaa.org
Phone: (240) 485-1001

Anxiety Disorders Foundation
Website: www.anxietydisordersfoundation.org
Email: info@anxietydisordersfoundation.org
Phone: (262) 567-6600

Association for Behavioral and Cognitive Therapies (ABCT)
Website: abct.org
Phone: (212) 647-1890

Bazelon Center for Mental Health Law
Website: bazelon.org
Email: info@bazelon.org
Phone: (202) 467-5730

College Living Experience
Website: cleinc.net
Phone: (800) 486-5058

Freedom from Fear
Website: www.freedomfromfear.org
Email: help@freedomfromfear.org
Phone: (718) 351-1717

Individuals with Disabilities Education Act (IDEA)
Website: http://idea.ed.gov
Phone: (202) 884-8215

International OCD Foundation
Website: ocfoundation.org
Email: info@ocfoundation.org
Phone: (617) 973-5801

Madison Institute of Medicine, Obsessive Compulsive Information Center
Website: miminc.org/aboutocic.asp
Email: mim@miminc.org
Phone: (608) 827-2470

National Alliance on Mental Illness
Website: nami.org
Phone: (800) 950-6264

National Institute of Mental Health
Website: nimh.nih.gov
Email: nimhinfo@nih.gov
Phone: (866) 615-6464

National Suicide Prevention Lifeline
Website: suicidepreventionlifeline.org
Phone: (800) 273-8255

Obsessive Compulsive Anonymous
Website: obsessivecompulsiveanonymous.org
Phone: (516) 739-0662

Partnership for Prescription Assistance
Website: www.pparx.org
Phone: (888) 477-2669

Peace of Mind Foundation
Website: peaceofmind.com
Email: info@peaceofmind.com

Substance Abuse and Mental Health Services Administration
Website: www.samhsa.gov
Phone: (877) 726-4727

Trichotillomania Learning Center (TLC)
Website: trich.org
Email: info@trich.org
Phone: (831) 457-1004

REFERENCES

Abramowitz, J. S. 2006. *Understanding and Treating Obsessive-Compulsive Disorder: A Cognitive-Behavioral Approach.* Mahwah, NJ: Lawrence Erlbaum Associates.

Allen, A. J., H. L. Leonard, and S. E. Swedo. 1995. Case study: A new infection-triggered, autoimmune subtype of pediatric OCD and Tourette's syndrome. *Journal of the American Academy of Child and Adolescent Psychiatry* 34(3):307–311.

Breslau, N., M. M. Kilbey, and P. Andreski. 1992. Nicotine withdrawal symptoms and psychiatric disorders: Findings from an epidemiologic study of young adults. *American Journal of Psychiatry* 149(4):464–469.

Carmody, T. P., C. Duncan, J. A. Simon, S. Solkowitz, J. Huggins, S. Lee, and K. Delucchi. 2008. Hypnosis for smoking cessation: A randomized trial. *Nicotine & Tobacco Research* 10(5):811–818.

Centers for Disease Control and Prevention. 2000. Cigarette smoking among adults in the United States, 1998. *Morbidity and Mortality Weekly Report (MMWR)* 49(39):881–884.

Chouinard, G. 1992. Sertraline in the treatment of obsessive-compulsive disorder: Two double-blind, placebo-controlled studies. *International Clinical Psychopharmacology* 7(Supplement 2):37–41.

Collaborative Study Group. 1991. Clomipramine in the treatment of patients with obsessive-compulsive disorder. *Archives of General Psychiatry* 48(8):730–738.

Crino, R. D., and G. Andrews. 1996. Obsessive-compulsive disorder and Axis I comorbidity. *Journal of Anxiety Disorders* 10(1):37–46.

Crum, R. M., and J. C. Anthony. 1993. Cocaine use and other suspected risk factors for obsessive-compulsive disorder: A prospective study with data from the Epidemiologic Catchment Area surveys. *Drug and Alcohol Dependence* 31(3):281–295.

Evins, A. E., M. A. Culhane, J. E. Alpert, J. Pava, B. S. Liese, A. Farabaugh, and M. Fava. 2008. A controlled trial of bupropion added to nicotine patch and behavioral therapy for smoking cessation in adults with unipolar depressive disorders. *Journal of Clinical Psychopharmacology* 28(6):660–666.

Gentil, A. F., M. A. de Mathis, R. C. Torresan, J. B. Diniz, P. Alvarenga, M. C. do Rosario, A. V. Cordioli, A. R. Torres, and E. C. Miguel. 2009. Alcohol use disorders in patients with obsessive-compulsive disorder: The importance of appropriate dual-diagnosis. *Drug and Alcohol Dependence* 100(1–2):173–177.

Goldstein, R. B., M. M. Weissman, P. B. Adams, E. Horwath, J. D. Lish, D. Charney, S. W. Woods, C. Sobin, and P. J. Wickramaratne. 1994. Psychiatric disorders in relatives of probands with panic disorder and/or major depression. *Archives of General Psychiatry* 51(5):383–394.

Green, R. C., and R. K. Pitman. 1991. Tourette syndrome and obsessive-compulsive disorder: Clinical relationship. In *Obsessive Compulsive Disorder: Theory and Management.* 2nd ed., edited by M. A. Jenike, L. Baer, and W. E. Minichiello. Chicago, IL: Yearbook Medical Publishers.

Greenberg, B. D., and A. R. Rezai. 2003. Mechanisms and the current state of deep brain stimulation in neuropsychiatry. *CNS Spectrums* 8(7):522–526.

Greist, J. H., J. W. Jefferson, K. A. Kobak, D. J. Katzelnick, and R. C. Serlin. 1995. Efficacy and tolerability of serotonin transport inhibitors in obsessive-compulsive disorder: A meta-analysis. *Archives of General Psychiatry* 52(1):53–60.

Harris, D. S., E. T. Everhart, J. E, Mendelson, and R. T. Jones. 2003. The pharmacology of cocaethylene in humans following cocaine and ethanol administration. *Drug and Alcohol Dependence* 72(2):169–182.

Insel, T. R., J. A. Hamilton, L. B. Guttmacher, and D. L. Murphy. 1983. D-Amphetamine in obsessive-compulsive disorder. *Psychopharmacology* 80(3):231–235.

Jaisoorya, T., Y. C. Janardhan/Reddy, and S. Srinath. 2003. The relationship of obsessive-compulsive disorder to putative spectrum disorders: Results from an Indian study. *Comprehensive Psychiatry* 44(4):317–323.

Jenike, M. A., L. Baer, H. T. Ballantine, R. L. Martuza, S. Tynes, I. Giriunas, M. L. Buttolph, and N. H. Cassem. 1991. Cingulotomy for refractory obsessive-compulsive disorder: A long-term follow-up of 33 patients. *Archives of General Psychiatry* 48(6):548–555.

Karno, M., J. Golding, S. Sorenson, and A. Burnam. 1988. The epidemiology of obsessive-compulsive disorder in five US communities. *Archives of General Psychiatry* 45(12):1094–1099.

Lasser, K., J. W. Boyd, S. Woolhandler, D. U. Himmelstein, D. McCormick, and D. H. Bor. 2000. Smoking and mental illness: A population-based prevalence study. *Journal of the American Medical Association* 284(20):2606–2610.

Mancebo, M. C., J. E. Grant, A. Pinto, J. L. Eisen, and S. A. Rasmussen. 2009. Substance use disorders in an obsessive compulsive disorder clinical sample. *Journal of Anxiety Disorders* 23(4):429–435.

Masi, G., S. Millepiedi, M. Mucci, N. Bertini, C. Pfanner, and F. Arcangeli. 2006. Comorbidity of obsessive-compulsive disorder and attention-deficit/hyperactivity disorder in referred children and adolescents. *Comprehensive Psychiatry* 47(1):42–47.

McCabe, S., C. Teter, and C. Boyd. 2006. Medical use, illicit use, and diversion of prescription stimulant medication. *Journal of Psychoactive Drugs* 38(1):43–56.

Morissette, S. B., M. T. Tull, S. B. Gulliver, B. W. Kamholz, and R. T. Zimering. 2007. Anxiety, anxiety disorders, tobacco use, and nicotine: A critical review of interrelationships. *Psychological Bulletin* 133(2):245–272.

National Institute on Drug Abuse. 2010. Prescription drug abuse—December 2010. *Topics in Brief* (December):1–2.

Nestadt, G., J. Samuels, M. A. Riddle, K.–Y. Liang, O. J. Bienvenu, R. Hoehn-Saric, et al. 2001. The relationship between obsessive-compulsive disorder and anxiety and affective disorders: Results from the Johns Hopkins OCD Family Study. *Psychological Medicine* 31(3):481–487.

Pauls, D. L., J. P. Alsobrook, W. Goodman, S. Rasmussen, and J. F. Leckman. 1995. A family study of obsessive-compulsive disorder. *American Journal of Psychiatry* 152(1):76–84.

Rasmussen, S. A., and J. L. Eisen. 1990. Epidemiology of obsessive compulsive disorder. *Journal of Clinical Psychiatry* 51(Suppl.):10–14.

Rasmussen, S. A., and M. T. Tsuang. 1986. Epidemiological and clinical findings of significance to the design of neuropharmacological studies of obsessive-compulsive disorder. *Psychopharmacological Bulletin* 22(3):723–729.

Sallet, P. C., P. G. de Alvarenga, Y. Ferrao, M. A. de Mathis, A. R. Torres, A. Marques, et al. 2010. Eating disorders in patients with obsessive-compulsive disorder: Prevalence and clinical correlates. *International Journal of Eating Disorders* 43(4):315–325.

Schruers, K., K. Koning, J. Luermans, M. J. Haack, and E. Griez. 2005. Obsessive-compulsive disorder: A critical review of therapeutic perspectives. *Acta Psychiatrica Scandinavica* 111:261-271

Skapinakis, P., T. Papatheodorou, and V. Mavreas. 2007. Antipsychotic augmentation of serotonergic antidepressants in treatment-resistant obsessive-compulsive disorder: A meta-analysis of the randomized controlled trials. *European Neuropsychopharmacology* 17:79-93

Steketee, G. S., J. Eisen, I. Dyck, M. Warshaw, and S. Rasmussen. 1999. Predictors of course in obsessive-compulsive disorder. *Psychiatry Research* 89(3):229–238.

Thornton, C., and J. Russell. 1997. Obsessive compulsive comorbidity in the dieting disorders. *International Journal of Eating Disorders* 21(1):83–87.

Weissman, M. M., R. C. Bland, G. J. Canino, S. Greenwald, H.–G. Hwu, C. Kyoon Lee, et al. 1994. The cross national epidemiology of obsessive compulsive disorder. *Journal of Clinical Psychiatry* 55(Suppl.):5–10.

Yaryura-Tobias, J., J. Todaro, M. S. Grunes, D. McKay, R. Stockman, and F. A. Neziroglu. 1996. Comorbidity versus continuum of Axis I disorders in OCD. Paper presented at the meeting of the Association for the Advancement of Behavior Therapy, New York, NY, November.

Zohar, J. and R. Judge. 1996. Paroxetine versus clomipramine in the treatment of obsessive-compulsive disorder: OCD Paroxetin Study Investigators. British Journal of Psychiatry 169: 468-474.

Michael A. Tompkins, PhD, specializes in the treatment of anxiety disorders. He is a founding partner of the San Francisco Bay Area Center for Cognitive Therapy and diplomate of the Academy of Cognitive Therapy. He is also assistant clinical professor at the University of California, Berkeley. He is author of *Digging Out*, was featured in the *New York Times* and the *Wall Street Journal*, and has appeared as a psychologist on TLC's *Hoarding: Buried Alive* and A&E's *Hoarders*. He lives in Oakland, CA.

Foreword writer **Jeff Bell** is author of *Rewind, Replay, Repeat: A Memoir of Obsessive-Compulsive Disorder*. He serves as a national spokesperson for the International OCD Foundation and is founder of the Adversity 2 Advocacy Project. Bell lives in Benicia, CA.

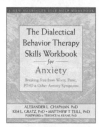